KITCHENS

Chris Casson Madden

KITCHENS

Photographs by Michael Mundy and John Vaughan

Research Assistance by Becky McDermott

Clarkson Potter/Publishers

New York

In memory of Grandma Casson—
in whose kitchen it all began

■ ■ ■ ■ ■ ■ ■ ■ ■ ■ ■ ■ ■ ■ ■ ■ ■ ■ ■ ■

Published by Clarkson N. Potter, Inc., 201 East 50th Street, New York, New York 10022. Member of the Crown Publishing Group.

Random House, Inc.
New York, Toronto, London, Sydney, Auckland

CLARKSON POTTER, POTTER, and colophon are trademarks of Clarkson N. Potter, Inc.

Manufactured in Japan

DESIGN BY GINA DAVIS

Library of Congress Cataloging-in-Publication Data
Madden, Chris Casson.
Kitchens / by Chris Casson Madden; photographs by Michael Mundy and John Vaughan.
Includes index.
1. Kitchens—United States.   2. Interior decoration—United States—History—20th century.   I. Title.
NK2117.K5M3   1993
747.7'97'097309048—dc20   92-16444

ISBN 0-517-58160-4
10 9 8 7 6 5 4 3 2

PHOTOGRAPH CREDITS

Michael Mundy: 5 (top left, bottom right); 6–9; 12; 13; 32–83; 85–93; 98–103; 112–115; 117; 126–151; 162-169; 174–186; 188–195; 200–207; 220–244; 245 (bottom); 246; 253, nos. 1–10; 255, nos. 1–9; 256, nos. 1–11, 13–15; 257, nos. 1–4, 6–8, 10–14, 17; 259, nos. 4–8, 10, 11, 13; 260, nos. 2, 5, 6, 9; 262, nos. 2, 11–13; 264, nos. 7, 12, 14; 265, nos. 1, 5, 6, 11; 266, nos. 5, 8, 10, 11; 267, no. 13; 269, nos. 2–5; 270, nos. 3–7, 9–11; 272, nos. 10–12; 275, nos. 1–5, 7–12; 276, nos. 1–14; 277, nos. 1–8; 277, nos. 3–8

John Vaughan: 5 (bottom left, top right); 2; 9 (bottom left): 10; 11; 14; 31; 84; 94–97; 104–111; 116; 152–161; 170–173; 180 (top right); 187; 196–199; 208–219, 245 (top); 252; 257, no. 16; 265, no. 9; 266, nos. 6, 7; 269, no. 1; 275, nos. 13–15

■ ■ ■ ■ ■ ■ ■ ■ ■ ■ ■ ■ ■ ■ ■ ■ ■ ■ ■ ■

Contents

Acknowledgments

I'd like first to offer a very special thanks and love to my husband, Kevin, who seems to make all things possible for me, and to my sons, Patrick and Nicholas, whose energy and joy keep me going forward, and to my parents and my brothers and sisters and their spouses for all their support.

I am especially grateful to John Vaughan, a dear friend and "photographer extraordinaire," who made each shoot an adventure in itself. Thanks also to Michael Mundy, Gina Mundy, and Scott Korn. Special gratitude goes to Becky McDermott, my friend, road companion, and invaluable associate, who always came through for me. The same gratitude goes to Julie Maher, my extraordinary assistant and traveling ace. Thanks also to Bobbie Kovsky for her many late nights of working with me and to Donna Mollica for helping to put the book "to bed."

This book could not have begun without the direction of my wonderful agent, Deborah Geltman, who brought me together with all the special people at Clarkson Potter: Carol Southern, whose unique editorial insight proved invaluable; Roy Finamore, my always patient and visionary editor; Bill Nave and Kristen Behrens, uncommon assistants who magically kept things running smoothly; Mark McCauslin; and Joan Denman. And a special thanks to a singular art director, Howard Klein. To all the people behind the scenes, including Mervyn Kaufman and Edwin F. Sierra—a huge vote of gratitude for everything you have done to make this book a reality. I'm also enormously appreciative of Gina Davis's great talents in designing *Kitchens*.

And, of course, I am indebted to my generous friends who graciously opened up their homes and their lives to me: Karin Blake, Ray and Roberta Beech, Arnelle Kase, Jennifer and James D'Auria, Robyn Low and Bran Ferren, Elizabeth and Fred Berry, Sally Quinn and Ben Bradlee, Steve and Cleves Weber, Thomas and Nan Rees, Barbara and Chip Waite, Craig Claiborne, Judy Licht and Jerry Della Femina, Larry and Diane Dunst, Thom Von Bulow, Helen Brandt, Anne and Patrick Lannan, Mariette and Raymond Gomez, Adrian Keller, Tina and Gerry Armstrong, Nancy McCabe, Lani and Larry Freymiller, Kitty Bartholomew, Nancy Heller, Lynn Von Kersting and Richard Irving,

Gennifer Witbeck, Alan Campbell, James Alan Smith, Gep Durenberger, Donna and Ken Fields, Sandy Slepak, Leslie King, Vanna Lacey, Carol and Nicky Paumgarten, Michael and Deborah Abrams, Kate and Charles Glennon, Friederike and Jeremy Biggs, Michael Ward, Jessica McClintock, Alice Waters, Julie Atwood, J. Allan Murphy, Detlef and Anna Pump, Phyliss and Lew Sugarman, Eva and Walter Iooss, Jr., Nan and Norm Rosenblatt, Teresa Heinz, Agnes Bourne and Jim Luebbers, Randy and Bunny Williams, Susan Freidland, George and Jenifer Lang, Phyllis Getzler, Andrée Putman, and André Bergos.

Behind the scenes are friends without whose help and advice I would not have been able to begin this project, especially Donna Truglio, Joan Vass, Charlotte Schoenfeld and Alison Greenberg of Charlotte Peters, Inc., Kevin Walsh, Michael Petrincola, Joyce MacRae, Nancy Novogrod and Carolyn Sollis, Frank Newbold, Stephanie Stokes, Jarluth and Neil Jacobs, Deborah Parsons of Terra Cotta, and Maria Gresham.

And appreciation to Amanda Berman, Pat Brunnelle, David Barrett, Susan Besher, Gary Crain, Melinda Blinker, Scott Bromley, Leola Macdonald, Kate Distan, Eric Berthold, Martin Filler, Dr. Andrew Gentile, Arsenio Gallegos, Ina Garten, Rela Gleason, Marva Griffen, David Gross, The Ivy Restaurant, Wanda Harris, Mark Hampton, Kitty Hawkes, Sarah Kaltman, Janie Kappes, Anne Keating, Deena Perry, Chris King, Christine Mather, Phillip Mazzurca, Mark Miller, Merle Miller, Leo Lerman, Jay Crawford, Danny Okrent, Louis Nicholson, Lydie Marshall, Myong Ok Heo, Patty Matson, Charles Patteson, Barbara Pohlman, Barbara Windom, Peter Piening, Carol Ryan, Dr. Sam Schwartz, Christopher Purvis, Lawrence Standish, Judy Sith, Rochelle Udell and Doug Turshen, Katherine Stephens, Mike Strohl, Steven Weaver, Vincent Wolf, Suzanne Varney, Paul Vincent Wiseman, Helen Barber, Calvin Fentress and Andy Schweitzer, Sean Driscoll, Carolyn Englefield, Susan Corsey, Frederick Stelle, Sheila de Rochambeau, Steven Reickart, the late Alex Gotfryd, Adam Tihany, Sirio Macchione, Tom Calloway, Steven Ball, Toni Gallagher, Sissy Eagan, Elin Vanderlip, Joan Lasker, Stephanie Fisher-Zernin. To *HG*, *Architectural Digest*, *House Beautiful*, and *Metropolitan Home* in appreciation of both your inspiration and cooperation, and finally a special thanks to the uplifting music of Eric Clapton, Brian Eno, Bonnie Raitt, Marvin Gaye, Steely Dan, Van Morrison, and Giacomo Puccini.

Introduction

Though my grandmother's kitchen did not have any of the multitude of labor-saving devices that I have in my own kitchen—or an efficient "triangle" layout—that room, more than any other I have been in, made me feel just like Colette's description: "in a state of happiness in advance of any years, a subtle happiness of satiated greed."

I especially recall the delicious aromas. Like Marcella Hazan's remembrance of the fruit from the perfumed orchards near her home in Bologna, Italy, and Craig Claiborne's reminiscence of the scents of celery, garlic, and parsley—"The Holy Trinity of Southern cooking"—in the Mississippi kitchen of his youth, Grandma Casson's kitchen summons up warm and rich memories for me today. She cooked casually but continuously, and her kitchen was open to whoever happened to be in the neighborhood.

That's not to say that I don't have fond memories of my mother's kitchen, too. I came from a large and wonderfully boisterous family of eleven. We'd gather at the kitchen table to eat and to discuss politics, report cards, and baseball scores, while my mother, who readily admits she is not a gourmet cook, seemed always to be in front of a very large pot of something splendid—a pot roast, maybe, or goulash, or her special pasta sauce. On mornings when my father wasn't concocting one of his countless efficiency charts for his nine children, he would whip up perfect bowls of Cream of Wheat, with a steaming pat of butter melting down into the center. But on weekends, I'd escape to my grandmother's house, with its flower gardens, goldfish ponds, and irresistible kitchen. There I was in heaven.

Then there was married life. Because of our careers—my husband, Kevin, is publisher of *HG* magazine, and I lecture and write about design—we have been fortunate to have eaten in some of the most special kitchens in the world, ranging from the "family table" at the famed Bice restaurant in Milan, Italy, to the late James Beard's kitchen in Greenwich Village. And because of these memories, when it came time to "do" my own kitchen, I wanted more than anything a place where family and friends could gather. I also wanted a reasonably efficient layout so on Saturday nights my husband and I could do what we truly enjoy—cook a feast together.

I decided to tackle our kitchen renovation myself. Faced with the major space constraints in our hundred-year-old home, I thought I didn't have much room to err. And as luck would have it, I didn't. After a year of intense research on my part—and help from James Davis, a great architect, for the entry and hall—the resulting kitchen plan is perfect for our two sons, a cocker spaniel, my husband, and myself.

I must confess, though, if I had to do it over, I would have used a kitchen planner or designer. A professional would have helped me through some major decisions quicker and easier, but in having to learn about those decisions and then make them, I also learned the ins and outs and ups and downs of kitchen planning.

What I did was take a small laundry room, a bathroom, and a very awkward kitchen that had been "fixed" in the 1960s and make them all into one long galley kitchen divided into two basic areas. The work space has everything you'd expect. The sitting area is anchored by a built-in desk and a bar sink; between them I placed our kitchen table with four cozy rattan chairs. Finding the right table wasn't easy. I went through two tables before we settled on a black circular table with two leaves that turn it into a long oval. It's the kind of table that immediately makes you want to sit down when you enter our kitchen.

Because I have a passion for order, I chose closed cupboards rather than open shelving, and I added as many built-ins, pull-outs, dividers, and special shelves as my budget allowed. Living with three men, I'm glad I did. There is, as I am wont to remind them, a place for everything.

I could not find room for an island or a fireplace, two items I did want (and still do)—but on the plus side, creative maneuvering on our architect's part added something else: a vista. We removed a wall and the door to our family room, which is seven steps below and beyond the kitchen. This not only opened an overflow sitting area for the kitchen, it also allowed us to see our back garden from the kitchen table. I still remember the first night Kevin and I sat down and looked out at the dahlias and lilies in our garden. We knew then it was worth every headache.

We are also fortunate in being able to watch the outside world pass by the front of our house from the large window by our kitchen table—a design take-off from the old front porches of years ago. And rather than block this view with curtains or shades, I just hung some of my collection of copper pots—twenty-seven of them to be exact—from a thick, strong iron bar with hooks across the top of the window frame. I had begun collecting these pots over twenty years ago; they have now found their perfect home.

ABOVE This kitchen is a gathering place for the kids and their friends.

BELOW My husband and I tried out a couple of tables in our kitchen before settling on this one.

ABOVE Removing a wall gave us access to the family room, which is several steps down from our kitchen.

BELOW A birdcage and some trailing plants over the sink take the place of a valance.

And although I am a professed neatnick, I *do* need to be surrounded by the old, offbeat, and somewhat whimsical kitchen tools that I search out in flea markets and antiques shops whenever we are on the road. My collections of potato mashers, antique molds, and vinegar bottles are all on display in this room.

I chose one appliance manufacturer—General Electric's Monogram line—because their glass came in black (my favorite accent color) and because I wanted to make one call, and only one call, for repairs. This decision has made life a lot easier—but that doesn't mean I don't sometimes look longingly at those big commercial numbers. What I've come to realize is that in kitchens, as with the rest of the rooms in your house, you must do what works for you.

Miscommunication between our contractor and myself led to the one major problem on the job. He assumed we were putting in a ¼-inch floor above the ¾-inch plywood, and he set in all the appliances. I had not yet decided on what type of flooring I wanted. Before we both realized the mistake, the deed was done. Appliances were in, allowing room for a floor of ¼ inch, and there went my dreams of limestone or chateau tile. (We would not be able to lift the dishwasher and refrigerator for repair over these thicker kinds of flooring.)

Since I wanted the kitchen to be more of an unobtrusive backdrop to the lively colors of food and people, I chose birch cabinets finished in pale whitewash. Off-white ceramic pulls from Italy blend in quietly. Apricot Jupirana granite, with some gray and black running throughout, forms our backsplash and makes me happy every time I see it. We had a young artist paint all the electric-outlet covers and switch plates in faux granite so they fade into the background.

High hats on dimmers and undercounter task lighting were put in each work area by one of the gems of this business—Richard Mecca, our electrician. He showed up when he said he would—this is a not-so-common occurrence in the construction business—discussed everything with me beforehand, and patiently explained why something was needed and where. I remain grateful to him.

With artwork by our children, friends, and relatives, our sons' height markings inside the pantry door, a comfortable chair, a "rainy day" cupboard filled with crayons, pipe cleaners, paints, and clay, and good memories of roller skating, Nerf football, and many little heads bobbing for apples each Halloween in this room, our kitchen surely is the sweet spot of our house.

When I set out to find the kitchens that you'll see on the following pages, I had two basic criteria: I wanted kitchens that were informational as well as inspirational. I wanted to capture the mood of the many special rooms that I've seen on my travels, but I also wanted to show you the nuts and bolts—pull-outs, secret compartments, tricks of the trade, and shortcuts—so that while you'd be considering your dream kitchen you'd also remember to put in such incidentals as a cabinet for recycling or a marble counter for rolling out pastry (if you are a baker) or an instant hot water dispenser or perhaps a wok stove (if you specialize in Chinese cooking). I searched also for kitchens that epitomized a more relaxed style and less formal design, one more true to one's own spirit.

These aren't just "work" rooms. Rather, they reflect the wonderful diversity of styles that permeates America today—styles as comfortable as a barely touched linoleum kitchen from the 1940s, as elegant as the late film director George Cukor's kitchen (recently updated by the owners of the hip Los Angeles restaurant The Ivy), or as eclectic as a kitchen where such luminaries as "Slim" Keith, John Saladino, and Mario Buatta would "hang out" and do dishes. I chose these kitchens for their authentic American spirit of individualism. I was also influenced by the marvelous creative use of natural elements coupled with the vast array of new technological developments that are making our own kitchen lives so much easier. In all these

kitchens both style and function triumph. The one constant I searched for in each was a sense of "soul"—life that goes beyond preparing meals and enriches the lives of all who enter.

I also wanted to help you in your own kitchen planning and design and decoration. This book is not just a compilation of beautiful workable kitchens that I've fallen in love with. Think of it as a practical jumping-off point. I've listed specifications and brand names for many of the products that I think might be of interest in each of the individual kitchen portraits in the front half of the book. The second half consists of a wide range of choices for flooring, appliances, lighting, cabinetry, extras (to give you an idea of what's out there or to provide you a new way to use a product that you might have never thought of before). Of course this listing cannot be all-inclusive, but it does let you know what's in store —with both popular and cutting-edge elements. This way, if you see some feature that you must have for your kitchen, you'll now know the brand, or if you love the look of a certain kitchen but think a different lighting might work better for you, you can just flip to the back lighting section and check out your other options.

It was a personally rewarding adventure to explore these great American kitchens and I hope you'll enjoy the journey as much as I did.

ABOVE The neutral hues of the counters and cabinets help highlight the bright colors of food.

BELOW Painted faux granite switch plates are less of an intrusion.

Classic

.... *Kitchens*
that bow to
well-honed
tradition

A Natural Setting

The owner had a very specific vision of what she wanted for the kitchen in her western Massachusetts home. With a hands-on enthusiasm for kitchen design, she researched the subject thoroughly and eagerly, emerging finally with a plan to create a room that highlighted wooden cabinets and a natural stone fireplace, rather than the clean white fixtures she had in mind when she first began her search for her "perfect" kitchen.

Working with architects Allan Shope and Bernard Wharton and designer Richard FitzGerald, the owners integrated certain specific features they required (such as the six-burner Wolf range and a "major" island) with some stunning effects. For instance, to hide the massive ducts and venting system and to keep a straight visual line over the Wolf range, artist James Alan Smith painted twelve trompe l'oeil panels that depict various kitchen scenes behind the "dummy" cabinet fronts. He also created the hand-painted checkerboard floor of coffee, butterscotch, and cream hues that unites prep and dining areas.

In the rehab process, the owner concluded that—as do most of us—she drew heavily on the past and on kitchens she had seen over the years. "There is nothing new under the sun. It's all a matter of compilation —how you put it all together. This room is interpreted through and for my personality and my needs. It's a big barn of a kitchen, and yet I still have that feeling I wanted, of warmth and intimacy."

Strong classic elements in a generously sized space are the keynotes of this striking kitchen. Grooved granite works effectively as a countertop drain; the pump-style fixture is imported from France.

ABOVE The black of the Windsor chairs around the kitchen table echoes the color of the Wolf stove beyond the granite-topped island.

ARCHITECTS: ALLAN SHOPE AND BERNARD
    WHARTON OF SHOPE RENO WHARTON
INTERIOR DESIGNER: RICHARD FITZGERALD
    AND ASSOCIATE GARY MCBOURNIE
TROMPE L'OEIL ARTIST: JAMES ALAN SMITH
CABINETS: FIR WOOD, CATO WOODWORK
COOKTOP: WOLF, SIX-BURNER
COUNTERTOPS: GRANITE
DISHWASHER: MIELE

FIXTURE: BILLIE BRENNER LTD.,
    BOSTON
GRILL: THERMADOR GAS GRILL
LIGHTING: LIGHTOLIER
OVENS: GAGGENAU; THERMADOR
PULLS: PERIOD FURNITURE HARDWARE,
    BOSTON
REFRIGERATOR-FREEZER: SUB-ZERO
SINK: BUTLER, ENGLAND

RIGHT A series of trompe l'oeil-on-glass
"cabinets" painted by James Alan
Smith disguises the venting system for
the stove.

ABOVE Firewood is dried and stored in the side opening of the massive stone fireplace.

OPPOSITE Large pantry pull-outs add accessible storage space.

ABOVE An antique game board hangs on a wall over the granite counter. Games are a theme in the decor throughout the house.

LEFT The Miele dishwasher, with its unique top shelf for knives, forks, and spoons, is conveniently located opposite the flatware drawer.

19

Convenience, with Views

A family of four (with two teenagers) wanted a multifunctional kitchen. As the owner pointed out, "We had to have a space that would suit our needs, from water fights to homework and everything in between. The children bring their friends home to hang out; we'll have close friends in for pizza; I'll do some repotting at the sink or sit at my computer to catch up." They also wanted a light, open space with all the latest kitchen features but without being "too ultra-modern."

Nan Rosenblatt, the designer who worked with the owners of this Dutch Colonial home in the Pacific Heights area of San Francisco, knew immediately that she wanted to transform three cramped rooms into one spacious "aerie." So, armed with a blueprint of the family's needs, Nan added a fireplace and a dining table that flips out to double its seating capacity, while taking full advantage of the marvelous views of the Golden Gate Bridge. By adding the massive Gothic-style skylight, she was able to tie the entire space together and at the same time bring light into the far corners of the room.

Because the house is traditional, Nan wanted to keep a traditional flavor in the kitchen. She did, while installing all the contemporary high-tech features on the market today: wire pull-out pantries, an "appliance shelf" that pops up and locks into place, two dishwashers, two sinks, lazy Susan corners in the cabinets, and a pop-up television set.

A Helian jade marble-topped center island holds a

A large Gothic-style skylight—with glass etchings executed by Eric Christianson—achieved the "aerie" feeling necessary to open up this room. The green wallpaper—"Winged Victory" from Anya Larkin—unites this large and irregular space.

Gaggenau grill, a recycling center, a garbage disposal, and a trash compactor. Nan's eye for meticulous detail is evident in the built-in Modern Maid toaster and the brass "yacht" hardware on the two cut-out recycling holes in the island.

Each work space was lit with downlights; soft ambient lighting by Halo was added throughout the rest of the room to simulate natural light as much as possible. The skylight allows natural light to come through, but at night, lighting placed six feet behind the etched glass continues this natural feeling.

General Electric's Monogram appliances in white were chosen for a uniform look to coordinate with the Poggenpohl cabinets. And, in order to keep it all from becoming too hard-edged, Nan formed a backdrop of textured wallpaper. Not only does it work well with the green marble island and countertops, it pulls this very large room together.

RIGHT Two sinks (one a double) and two dishwashers are both convenient and efficient. Hidden below the circular cut-outs in the island are a compactor and trash receptacle—practical solutions to disposing counter waste.

BELOW The dining area was designed to capture the view of the Golden Gate Bridge. Tableware from Sue Fisher King's shop in San Francisco and a tabletop topiary add to the natural theme.

ABOVE A miniature twig chair is used to decorate the counter above a double lazy Susan corner cabinet.

RIGHT Designed for maximum storage and accessibility, the wire pull-out pantry slides in and out easily.

BELOW "Open Sesame," a remote-control device from the Hafele Company, operates the system that raises and lowers the television set and video cassette recorder. The TV is covered with a slab of the same green marble as the counter, helping it disappear completely.

ARCHITECT: Reginald Van Pelt of Nan Rosenblatt Interior Design
INTERIOR DESIGNER: Nan Rosenblatt
CONTRACTOR: Paragon
APPLIANCE SHELF: Poggenpohl
CABINETS: Poggenpohl, white high-gloss polyester
COOKTOP: General Electric "Monogram"
COUNTERTOP: Marble
DISHWASHERS: General Electric "Monogram"
FIXTURES: Franke

FLOOR: bleached white oak
GLASS ARTISAN: Eric Christianson
GRILL: Gaggenau
LIGHTING: Halo
OVEN: General Electric "Monogram"
RECYCLING FIXTURES: boating fixtures
REFRIGERATOR: General Electric "Monogram"
SINKS: Elkay
WALLS: Anya Larkin textured wallpaper
WIRE PANTRIES: Poggenpohl

OPPOSITE A pop-up shelf locks into place, providing additional work space for blenders and food processors. When not in use, the shelf stores conveniently underneath the island. The Gaggenau grill set into the island is vented through the flooring. The wall toaster is from Modern Maid.

Tradition Reinterpreted

· ·

Only two objects remain today from the original 1926 design of this kitchen: the massive black stove hood and the "Rube Goldberg" venting system that runs above it. Other than that, the three rooms—kitchen, butler's pantry, and breakfast nook—were completely renovated in a collaborative effort by the owner and his designer, Stephanie Stokes.

The owner, a bachelor who loves to cook, believed that his kitchen must keep within the style of the apartment, while being up to date. The original premise was to preserve as much of the kitchen as possible, but the more practical route held sway: duplicating the style of the cabinetry and the overall sense of the kitchen. "It was a total gut job," remembers the owner. "The cabinets looked great, but they were in all the wrong places."

With a reading lamp and chairs pulled up next to the windowsill, there is an inviting sense to this room, yet practicality abounds. Kick-out baseboards around the perimeter of the room conceal extra storage; a wooden ladder moves around the room on its own brass runner to allow access to storage high overhead (space wasted in many other kitchens). Additional illuminated work areas were created by adding incandescent lighting strips under the counters. And a mirrored backsplash creates the sense of more open space.

High ceilings in the apartment enabled the owner to hang the pot rack, custom made by Frombruche, directly over the work area—within reach but high enough to avoid heads.

At left, a plaid easy chair—one of a pair covered in a Brunschwig & Fils fabric—adds a note of country to this practical city kitchen. At right, the owner retained the huge hood from the original kitchen but added a six-burner Wolf range. Tinned spices are within easy reach.

ARCHITECT/DESIGNER: STEPHANIE STOKES, INC.

CONTRACTOR: TACONIC BUILDERS

BACKSPLASH: MIRROR

BASEBOARD STORAGE: FABRICATED BY TACONIC BUILDERS, DESIGNED BY STEPHANIE STOKES

BRASS RAIL SYSTEM: COLONIAL BRASS WORKS

CABINETS: PAINTED MAPLE, FABRICATED BY TACONIC BUILDERS, DESIGNED BY STEPHANIE STOKES

COUNTERTOP: GRANITE

DISHWASHERS: GENERAL ELECTRIC

FIXTURES: CHICAGO

FLOOR: WALNUT AND WHITE OAK

LADDER: FABRICATED BY TACONIC BUILDERS

LIGHTING: CASE INCANDESCENT UNDER-COUNTER STRIP LIGHTING, FROMBRUCHE BRASS AND PEWTER OVERHEAD LIGHTING

POT RACK: CUSTOM-MADE BY FROMBRUCHE

PULLS: BALDWIN BRASS

REFRIGERATOR/FREEZER: SUB-ZERO

SINK: FRANKE

STOVE: WOLF

WINE COOLER: KEDCO

LEFT By extending the top of the granite island, the designer created an informal eating counter; the stools underneath it are from the ocean liner *Normandie*. A pot rack overhead was custom built to the size of the island.

BELOW New cabinets have a vintage look. The mirrored backsplash adds an element of surprise while visually increasing the size of the room. Strip lighting beneath the cupboards provides important task lighting.

ABOVE The slice in the top of the granite island is designed for knife storage. The Chicago fixture is convenient for washing large items.

BELOW LEFT Every inch of space in this room has been thought out for maximum usage. Kick-out baseboards offer additional yet well-hidden storage.

OPPOSITE A ladder on a brass runner helps the owner reach deep cupboard storage. The pantry-bar area duplicates the design ambience of the kitchen.

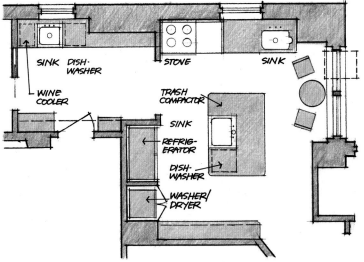

SINK DISH-WASHER

STOVE

SINK

WINE COOLER

TRASH COMPACTOR

SINK

REFRIG-ERATOR

DISH-WASHER

WASHER/ DRYER

Romantic Modernism

Some men have been known to buy a speedboat or sports car to relax. James D'Auria built a dream kitchen. James, an architect by profession, and Jennifer, his actress wife, had been living in a former stables in Bridgehampton, Long Island, for a number of years before they took on the task of redoing their kitchen. "We lived with it for such a long time," he says. "We entertained more and I became involved in cooking and food. The living room wasn't the answer to our space needs. What we wanted was a place where friends could all gather round and enjoy themselves while Jennifer and I were enjoying ourselves."

James's architectural designs are in the classical tradition, but with a sense of modernism. "The idea of making simple shapes that have strong form really became the dominating force behind the whole concept," he explains. "We have so many French doors, I was worried that the kitchen would become too cute, too sentimental, so the architecture of the room is simple but romantic."

Materials were chosen for their clarity and their hard edges, again combining modernism with tradition. The floor, for example, is a heavy natural stone with a very irregular edge. The D'Aurias added a few steps at the exterior end of the room so that this space would integrate more closely with the outdoors. The cabinets and the backsplash—all designed by James—are of anigre wood bleached to add a subtle texture. The marble island top is another instance of employing an element that was hard and clean, and yet in time would become worn and reassuringly familiar.

French doors and a nine-paned circular window bring the outdoors inside this summer house kitchen. The stone floor and linen slipcovers are informal yet modern.

ARCHITECT: JAMES D'AURIA
BUILDER: BEN KRUPINSKI
CABINETS AND BACKSPLASH: BLEACHED
    ANIGRE DESIGNED BY JAMES
    D'AURIA, FABRICATED BY MEAD &
    JOSIPOVICH
CHAIRS: DESIGNED BY JAMES D'AURIA
    FOR PROMEMORIA (LECCO, ITALY)
COUNTERTOP: ARABESCATO MARBLE
DISHWASHER: KITCHENAID
FIXTURES: CHICAGO
FLOOR: NATURAL STONE "CRAB
    ORCHID"
GRILL: JENN-AIR
LIGHTING: LIGHTOLIER AND ALKO
REFRIGERATOR/FREEZER: SUB-ZERO
SINK: FRANKE, STAINLESS-STEEL ELKAY
STOVE: VIKING

OPPOSITE The well-worn nine-foot-long French pine table dates from the eighteenth century and is flanked by eight chairs designed by D'Auria. The understated floral linen slipcover fabric is by Bennison.

BELOW A hooded Viking stove and a Jenn-Air grill set into the counter are used for winter barbecuing.

ABOVE The clean curve of the marble-topped island, along with the sleekness of the refrigerator, adds a counterpoint to the uneven edges of the stone floor. All were designed to withstand hard wear and tear.

Hollywood Restoration

Created from several small rooms, the Hollywood Hills kitchen of Lynn von Kersting and Richard Irving still retains the Old World elegance that prevailed during Hollywood's "golden years." Originally the home of film director George Cukor, the house to this day has the enchantment and feel of Cukor's stage sets but has its own character and sensibility.

In relaxed residence now after the house's year of renovation, Richard Irving is the chef behind three popular Los Angeles institutions—The Ivy, The Ivy at the Shore, and L.A. Desserts. Lynn is responsible for the magic at her own design firm and Indigo Seas, the quintessential design source shop.

Richard's goal was that the kitchen in his home would be as efficient as the kitchen he was building for his restaurant, while maintaining the panache and glamour that the Cukor heritage bestowed.

First, efficiency. In the center of the room they installed an oversized butcher block–topped island with electric outlets and great undercounter cupboards that hold everything from a pull-out trash container to a potholder drawer. The walk-around space is generous. A built-in pantry opens to reveal swing-out, multitiered shelving and inside every drawer can be found efficiently divided sections.

Second, panache and glamour. The black-and-white diamond-pattern ceramic tile floor is elegant and sophisticated, yet it was chosen for its durability; and the pungent yellow walls are the perfect backdrop

This spacious room was originally the kitchen, sewing room, and laundry. The center island is topped with a durable maple butcher block. Potted plants and a massive bouquet of rosemary contribute to the garden theme, while the garlands of red peppers hanging from the beams were a housewarming present from Sophia Loren.

ABOVE Black tole trays and bamboo side chairs—all from the Indigo Seas shop—contrast with the egg-yolk yellow walls.

OPPOSITE The Irish sideboard serves as a stage for the ever-changing display of flowers and vegetables from Richard's garden. The painted coffee urn is an antique.

ABOVE Pieces from Lynn's collection of Staffordshire plates frame the kitchen's back door.

BELOW Lynn's personal touch is evident everywhere. A silver cup and trophy on an eighteenth-century French country desk are elegant catchalls for everyday paraphernalia.

for Lynn's collection of nineteenth-century Tole trays.

This kitchen bears the stylish stamp that Lynn brings to every project she is involved in. From the nineteenth-century Irish sideboard, which houses her collection of Staffordshire plates and a Victorian papier-mâché samovar, to the eighteenth-century French country desk laden with old Venetian glass, every aspect of the kitchen reflects Lynn's peripatetic search for great objects.

Although the kitchen's book-lined wall houses hundreds of volumes on cooking and gardening, and it is the room where Richard experiments with new recipes for their restaurants, it is also, most decidedly, a room for relaxation. "We listen to music, and read to our little girl, India," says Lynn. "It's so irresistible a place that Ricky is able to switch gears from the restaurants and be quite happy cooking here. We love to sit around the table with a simple pasta of fresh basil and tomato from the garden and a bottle of wine."

As in so many southern California homes, the gardens are an integral part of the kitchen life. "Richard and my mother, Patou, are wonderful gardeners, and most of the flowers, herbs, fruits, and vegetables used in the restaurants—as well as for the house—are grown in our gardens, which creates a magical backdrop for our poolside kitchen."

ABOVE A water spigot was installed next to the Viking stove so water for pots of pasta is within reach.

RIGHT The ceramic tile floor is Italian. A skylight brightens what would have been a dark corner.

INTERIOR DESIGNER: INDIGO SEAS, INC.
COUNTERTOP: CERAMIC TILE AND
    BUTCHER BLOCK
DISHWASHER: KITCHENAID
FIXTURES: CHICAGO
FLOOR: CERAMIC TILE
ICEMAKER: ADMIRAL
LIGHTING: SKYLIGHT; HALOGEN;
    RECESSED HIGH HATS; INCANDESCENT
    UNDERCOUNTER LIGHTS
REFRIGERATOR: SUB-ZERO
SINK: ELKAY
STOVE: VIKING
WALLS: EGG-YOLK YELLOW

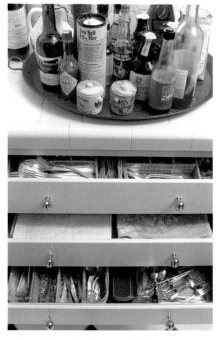

ABOVE Wicker baskets stylishly separate the silverware and other utensils. Condiments are kept on a lazy Susan.

ABOVE Custom-built pantry doors have narrow shelves that swing out, making it easier to keep track of grocery items.

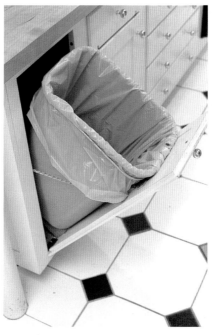

ABOVE A strategically placed trash container pulls out on an angle.

BELOW The kitchen is equipped with many shelves, which allows Lynn and Richard to buy and store in bulk.

BELOW One of the kitchen's many narrow drawers is used to store potholders and placemats.

ABOVE One wall is given over to the couple's eclectic and much-used collection of cooking and gardening books.

RIGHT Fresh flowers from the owners' gardens are a constant in the design scheme of this kitchen. Comfortable rush chairs surround the nineteenth-century Irish dining table.

OVERLEAF At left is a view of the butler's pantry, with the dining room in the background. At right, garden roses fill a water-glass, martini shaker, and small pitcher in a spare corner of a kitchen counter.

Poolside Kitchen

This small changing room near the pool was transformed into a working kitchen with the basics: an apartment-sized refrigerator, dishwasher, and large icemaker. Old Portuguese tiles line the walls.

Close by is an outdoor wood-burning oven where the owners roast fresh fish and bake bread, a rotisserie for cooking turkey and chicken on the spit, and an enormous barbeque built for them in Mesquite, Texas, for grilling meat and fresh vegetables from the surrounding gardens. This is southern California outdoor entertaining at its most sublime.

OPPOSITE A "porthole" frames a view from the garden into the small outdoor kitchen and patio dining area.

RIGHT An old poolside changing room was converted into a simple outdoor kitchen—complete with sink, stove, refrigerator, and cabinets.

BELOW A custom-built wood-burning oven is used for baking garlic and rosemary-scented bread. The barbecue next to it was built in Mesquite, Texas.

Bricks and Tiles

The weekend retreat of New York advertising executive Larry Dunst and his wife, Diane, is a classic Dutch Colonial cottage, built in 1899 in East Hampton, Long Island. When they restored the house in the late 1980s, the Dunsts were determined that the kitchen would reflect the extraordinary and vivid range of colors and light that are the hallmark of the changing seasons in eastern Long Island. "We wanted to bring the outside in, to take advantage of that marvelous light," said Diane. So three pairs of French doors were added to create additional light sources for the kitchen. They gained more space by opening up a pantry, then created a separate breakfast room where a mud room formerly stood. The original cooking fireplace, discovered behind a brick wall during renovation, has been restored and is now one of the highlights of this room.

Larry and Diane intentionally used pieces that one might not expect to see in a kitchen, such as the small Chinese rugs from the 1920s, the English Regency antique desk, and the George III hanging oak cabinet. But with Diane's intense interest in things culinary, the real star of the kitchen is the Crown stove. "With its six burners and two ovens, it has the versatility of a restaurant stove," says Diane, "but it's smaller and easier to work with. Our feelings about restaurant stoves in the home is that they're great decorating statements, but practically speaking, they're called restaurant stoves for a good reason. They belong in restaurants."

Sanderson's "Lansdowne" paper covers the kitchen walls. The small cabinet holds Larry and Diane's collection of antique napkin rings—each inscribed with a name.

ARCHITECT/DESIGNER: LARRY AND DIANE
     DUNST
CONTRACTOR: BEN KRUPINSKI
COUNTERTOP AND BACKSPLASH: CORIAN
DISHWASHER: THERMADOR
FIXTURES: CHICAGO
FLOOR: VILLEROY & BOCH CERAMIC
     TILE
LIGHTING: LIGHTOLIER
POT RACK: CUSTOM PAINTED BY BRIAN
     LEAVER
REFRIGERATOR/FREEZER: SUB-ZERO
SINK: ELKAY
STOVE: CROWN SIX-BURNER, DOUBLE-
     OVEN, GAS
WALLS: SANDERSON "LANSDOWNE"
     WALLPAPER

OPPOSITE Green shelves over the restored brick cooking fireplace are convenient for storing a collection of copper pots.

BELOW The small 1920s Chinese rug is one of four scattered throughout the kitchen.

ABOVE French bistro bar stools, purchased on a trip to Paris, flank the Corian-covered center island. The crisp-looking ceramic floor tile is by Villeroy & Boch.

Rustic

.... *Six kitchens*
that pay tribute
to the world
outside their
windows

Spirited Eclecticism

Lani and Larry Freymiller—perhaps more than most people—celebrate the home and the kitchen and relish sharing their spacious surroundings with friends and family. Whether it is dying Easter eggs, baking Christmas cookies, or hosting a summer wedding, the Freymillers love to entertain, and they have designed the kitchen in their Rancho Santa Fe, California, home to accommodate company. A large work island, three sinks (including ones in the bar and pantry), a butcher-block table, a Viking stove, and a Sub-Zero refrigerator leaves them well equipped.

Butcher-block countertops were built extra high to accommodate Larry's height. The area around the sink is covered in white tiles. The walls are rough-sawn cedar, sprayed with water-based Navaho white paint, which brings out the yellow tones of the wood. The cabinets are old but have been rearranged and refinished in a faux rustic patina, which adds the texture the Freymillers were looking for.

The spaciousness of the kitchen also enables the Freymillers to mix—with a spirited eclecticism—the styles of the Southwest with Victorian teapots, antique linens, primitive birdhouses, country furniture, folk art, quilts, and pottery. The southern California climate and the space of the kitchen also allows them to indulge their passion for growing herbs.

When the Freymillers completed their renovation, they had succeeded in opening up the kitchen to the outside, particularly the garden. "In the summer all the doors are open," says Lani, "and the kitchen becomes the heart of the party."

One of the three sinks overlooks the garden and is framed by the neutral colors of earthenware, baskets, and crockery.

55

ABOVE Although this room is only three years old, the profusion of dried herbs, peppers and garlic, and carefully selected accessories makes it look like a room with a past.

BUILDER: JON O'BRIEN
CABINETS: EXISTING, WITH FAUX FINISH
    BY JASON CALL
COUNTERTOP: BUTCHER BLOCK
DISHWASHER: THERMADOR
FLOOR: AMERICAN KRAFT TILES
LIGHTING: HIGH HATS
REFRIGERATOR: SUB-ZERO
SINK: ELKAY
SINK SURROUND: WHITE FLORIDA TILES
STOVE: VIKING
WALLS: WHITE-WASHED ROUGH-SAWN
    CEDAR

OPPOSITE A *metate*—a stone originally used by Native Americans to grind corn—has been transformed into a cookbook holder next to the stove.

RIGHT This work counter has been built higher than standard because Larry is tall. Understated white ceramic pulls were chosen to accent the newly painted but old-looking cabinet fronts.

ABOVE With a carefully chosen mélange of pieces, this room reflects the eclectic spirit of the whole house. Dinner for four can be around the sofa in front of the fireplace, at the square kitchen table, or—during warmer summer months—in the outdoor garden beyond.

BELOW LEFT Inexpensive rough-sawn cedar planks were spray painted and used as paneling on walls and ceiling.

BELOW Earthenware mugs from Mexico are stored in a basket on the floor.

ABOVE A terra-cotta wine rack is cooled by a cold-water pipe in the rear.

BELOW The Elkay sink has been fitted with a dish-soap dispenser.

ABOVE A collection of charming old birdhouses transforms a corner. The old trough under the table is used to store vegetables.

A Touch with Tin

"I knew at first sight that the bones of the house were extraordinary," says Anne Lannan of the hundred-year-old "pueblo-style" home that she and her husband, Patrick, restored. Over the years, the house had lost some of the elements characteristic of its traditional adobe, so with the help of architect Richard Martin, the Lannans set out to recapture its original integrity.

They made some basic cosmetic and structural changes: the beams, or "vigas," were sanded down to their natural color; the refrigerator was moved; a rounded wall was added for warmth; and the window seat in the dining area was deepened so that it became a haven for lolling about, reading, and planning menus. Because the Lannans did not want to rework the plumbing, they kept the sink where it was. Everything in this kitchen is organized, down to the alphabetical arrangement of the spices. "You have to admit, it's a lot easier to find things if you know where they are," says Anne.

A visit to a friend's kitchen provided the inspiration for this kitchen's signature: imaginative metalwork. Robert Stanfield, one of the leading practitioners of this little-known art, aged new tin in an intricate process and applied it over the preexisting German cabinetry to achieve the patina that the Lannans desired. Designer Karin Blake helped Anne with the finishing touches. She found the hickory chairs and tracked down some Sabino pieces like the counter and the dining table (from Claiborn Gallery and Dewey Gallery, both in Santa Fe).

The long runner helps define the work area of the kitchen. A ceiling fan has been set in between the vigas.

ABOVE Application of aged and intricately patterned tinwork has dramatically transformed the cabinet fronts.

ARCHITECT: RICHARD MARTIN
INTERIOR DESIGNER: KARIN BLAKE
BACKSPLASH: TILE
CABINETS: FRONTS CUSTOM FABRICATED
   BY ROBERT STANFIELD
COOKTOP: U.S. RANGE
COUNTERTOP: FORMICA, EDGED IN WOOD
DISHWASHER: MAYTAG
FLOOR: WIDE-WOOD PLANKS
LIGHTING: TRACK
OVEN: KITCHENAID
REFRIGERATOR: AMANA 23 ENERGY
   SAVER
TIN WORK: ROBERT STANFIELD
WALLS: STUCCO

ABOVE An old breadbox is a bit of kitchenalia that helps set the tone of the room.

BELOW Scattered randomly throughout the backsplash are tiles with a pressed sprig pattern.

OPPOSITE A large opening in the side of the U.S. Range is ideal for storing oversized baking sheets.

BELOW The original German cabinetry provides generous storage space.

A Reworked Barn

Ken and Donna Fields's lifelong dream was to live in a barn. After a long, sometimes circuitous search, they found one that they liked in New England and had it moved to a parcel of land situated in the center of the northern California's San Padre National Forest. Each piece of wood was numbered and put back together by the same workers who dismantled the structure.

The kitchen was designed to blend into this interior space—never to stand out. The challenge was to disguise the kitchen appliances as much as possible without sacrificing modern conveniences—in short, to achieve an "unindustrial" look.

The couple decided not to stain or paint the two-hundred-year-old wood. The finish is the mellowed result of years of hay rubbing against wood. The patina of the lower cabinets is again old wood; their architect, Dan Dickson, found old kitchen cabinets in a nearby home that dated back to the 1920s. The configuration and color weren't exactly what the Fieldses had in mind, but they felt that these rather old pieces of wood might blend in with the barn. Dickson reworked, stripped, and lightly sandblasted the cabinets—then custom stained them to match the barn siding. Reproduction Shaker knobs on all the cabinets were also stained to match. The wooden shelves and bullnose edging on the tile counters are old wood, too—the same vintage as the rest of the barn.

The hidden surprise here is solar energy, which is what keeps everything humming and running smoothly at the Fieldses' home. A bank of batteries and solar panels in a nearby storage shed brings the sun's energy through solar wires into the timeless kitchen.

Open to the rest of the converted barn, this kitchen has become the heart of the home.

ABOVE The backsplash is indigo and white stoneware tile, set in a typically American checkerboard pattern. Notice that even the front panel of the dishwasher is cloaked in the old wood.

RIGHT The commercial porcelain sink was fitted with a Horus faucet that looks old.

OPPOSITE A Thermador cooktop sits atop old wooden cabinets that date back to the 1920s. The wood of the cabinets was custom stained to match the patina of the barn walls.

RIGHT The countertop is white tile with intentionally darkened grout. It is trimmed with barn wood.

ABOVE An iron stagecoach doorstop—perhaps a symbol of the barn's trek—is displayed on a kitchen sill.

LEFT Hidden behind an antique door with its original green paint is the solar-energized refrigerator.

OPPOSITE The bar stools are from Richard Mulligan's shop in Los Angeles. The one in the foreground is an antique, the other a reproduction. The American wool braided rug is from the late nineteenth century.

ARCHITECT: DAN DICKSON
INTERIOR DESIGNER: DONNA FIELDS
CARPENTER: MARK SAUNDERS
BACKSPLASH: INDIGO AND WHITE
 STONEWARE TILE MADE BY BUSBY-
 GILBERT WITH ORIGINAL BEAMS
CABINETS: SALVAGE
COOKTOP: THERMADOR
COUNTERTOP: BUSBY-GILBERT WHITE
 TILE TRIMMED WITH BARN WOOD
DISHWASHER: IN-SINK-ERATOR
FIXTURE: "JULIA" BY HORUS
FLOOR: ORIGINAL ANTIQUE BARN FLOOR
LIGHTING: NIGHTSCAPING
OVEN: GAGGENAU
PULLS: REPRODUCTION SHAKER
REFRIGERATOR: SUN-FROST COVERED BY
 AN ANTIQUE DOOR WITH ORIGINAL
 GREEN PAINT
SINK: COMMERCIAL PORCELAIN
WALLS: PLASTER SUPPORTED BY
 ORIGINAL BARN BEAMS

Pioneer Ambience

Located on 360 acres in the center of New Mexico's Rio Chama wilderness area, the home of Fred and Elizabeth Berry has what seems more like an 1800s pioneer kitchen than a room built just a few years ago —but the building process was almost as primitive as in the days of the early homesteaders.

The Berrys have no electricity, no gas lines, no telephone. They made the three thousand adobe bricks for inside and outside the concrete shell themselves. And since the ranch is two hours from anywhere by a very rough dirt road, everything from the grand piano to the propane refrigerator had to be trucked in on the back of their pickup.

Elizabeth's mother was a source of inspiration for the kitchen details. An addicted clipper of how-to articles, she came up with such practical ideas as the pull-out cutting boards in the china cupboard, the wooden pull-out dowels for the tablecloths, and the dividers for storing serving trays and oversized pans.

Most of the decorative pieces in the kitchen have been in Elizabeth's family for generations, and along with the faded black-and-white photographs of her ancestors, they give a special feel to this room. Lighting after sunset is all by candlelight.

Even though it is not an easy trek to get to the Berry ranch, such food luminaries as Mark Miller, Larry Forgione, and Jonathan Waxman have all spent time here —picking Elizabeth's crops and cooking up a storm in either her indoor or outdoor kitchen.

The brick floor, the adobe and plaster walls, and the simple pine cabinets all pay homage to the pioneer heritage of this home in the New Mexican mountains. The shortwave radio on the butcher-block chopping board is the only source of communication with the outside world.

ABOVE Mexican tile is used to cover the countertop. The ceiling is a "Latilla," a traditional southwestern technique.

OPPOSITE Lighting is all by candlelight. An heirloom silver chandelier that can be raised and lowered by a chain pulley hangs over the kitchen table. The Elmira Sweetheart wood-burning stove is used both for cooking meals and heating the house.

RIGHT Old silver and photographs are set out on the kitchen dresser.

ARCHITECT: BOB STRADER, JR.
BUILDER: THOMAS HEINRITZ
CABINETMAKER: FRANK MOXAM
COUNTERTOP: MEXICAN TILE
FLOOR: BRICK
LIGHTING: CANDLES
REFRIGERATOR: SIBIR PROPANE
STOVE: MAGIC CHEF AND ELMIRA
  SWEETHEART, WOOD-BURNING
WALLS: PLASTER

■ ■

Outdoor Kitchen

Outside the Berry ranch in New Mexico is a second, very necessary "kitchen." This structure is not only used as the headquarters for the harvest of crops that Elizabeth Berry grows for the Coyote Café and other well-known Santa Fe restaurants, it is also where much of the cooking is done in the summer to keep the interior kitchen cool (twenty-two-inch-thick adobe walls have a tendency to hold the heat).

Cooking is done either by propane three-burner cooktop or a "horno," a wood-burning adobe oven sealed with mud. Water is delivered by a gravity-flow system from a spring a quarter of a mile away.

TOP LEFT In the background of the Berry Ranch are thousand-foot sandstone cliffs once used by Anasazi Indians as lookout towers. "When I'm out here," says Berry, "I feel totally centered—totally integrated with nature."

LEFT Organic produce harvested from the gardens is prepared for market on linoleum-covered tables in the outdoor kitchen. Pots hang from nails hammered into the roof. The sink is homely, but serviceable.

ABOVE A sloping galvanized-steel roof covers the outdoor kitchen, which contains the three-burner propane cooktop and a hand-pumped water faucet. A tree trunk doubles as a support post and a pot rack.

Southwestern
Sophistication

Helen Brandt came up with a very simple solution to a fairly common syndrome: How to get her husband into her favorite room, the kitchen. "For years I've been trying to coax him into spending more time in the kitchen, but with little success. So, early on, while we were still in the building stages, we made him a personalized seating area right next to the hearth. We actually had him try it out, and we molded the adobe to his body. The whole idea was to get him to feel so relaxed and comfortable that he'd find himself hard put to leave."

Perched high in the mountains and mesas of New Mexico, the Brandt house's kitchen strongly reflects its roots—from the adobe and the carved "lightning" and "cloud" designs on the cabinet fronts and striking wrought-iron pot rack to the collection of brown Navaho pottery atop the refrigerator and ovens. Lila DeWindt, an architect in Brandt's office, handled all the detailing for the kitchen. It was she who suggested these traditional New Mexican designs and carried them into the cabinetry throughout.

The unusual sage color scheme was not inspired, as one might expect, by the view of the mesa from the kitchen sink: It had a much more practical inspiration —the Thermador line of blue-green appliances that the owners found and soon decided to use as a color scheme for the entire room.

The meticulously thought-out space in the Brandt kitchen is the secret to what makes it all work. Because this room is the hub, the practical and aesthetic spatial planning had to be absolutely perfect.

At left, an Avonite center island has a "bridge" added to the middle, creating additional storage and show space. At right, the "lightning" cutouts are backed with reflective glass.

ABOVE The stainless-steel Franke sink was chosen to blend with the muted sage color of the cabinets and not to break the long expanse of the Avonite surface. Deer antlers are used as a towel hook.

LEFT The single-spout fixture has been placed in the corner rather than the center of the sink.

ABOVE Convenient and safe, the knife drawer allows the cook to keep sharp knives within reach yet out of sight.

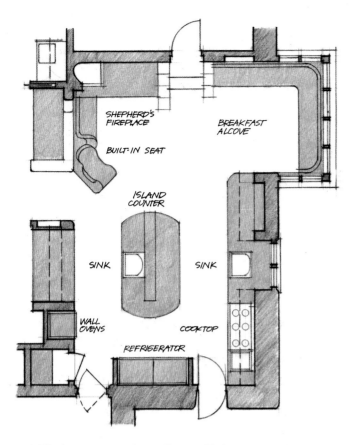

SHEPHERD'S FIREPLACE

BREAKFAST ALCOVE

BUILT-IN SEAT

ISLAND COUNTER

SINK   SINK

WALL OVENS   COOKTOP

REFRIGERATOR

"We have guests here," says Helen, "and the layout was planned with informal entertaining in mind." Helen discovered that in planning a kitchen with a Sub-Zero refrigerator and freezer, one must consider clearance space for the massive doors. The center island with the requisite second sink is the anchor for the work zone but has plenty of walk-around space. The relaxed seating area near the fireplace adds another dimension. The well-organized storage space, which helps keep the countertops free from clutter, is found behind cabinets, in slide-out drawers, under counters, and in three well-situated appliance garages. Helen found that people love to be involved in the kitchen. "Everyone gravitates to this room. Not only can it handle them, but I believe that when guests are in the kitchen, whether zipping around and helping out or watching it all come together, it makes them feel more actively involved in the rest of the house."

To integrate all the areas, the Brandts laid a gray and greenish-blue slate floor, which unites the dining, work, and serving areas visually. The speckled desert hues of the Avonite countertop pull the island and the eighteen-foot-long counter perceptively together.

ABOVE Custom panels were created from Alaskan cedar to cover the fronts of the Sub-Zero refrigerator and freezer. The curved corners of the counter and undershelves create a softer look and offer extra display space.

ABOVE The appliance garage puts an end to countertop clutter, while allowing machines for related tasks to be grouped together. A strip electric bar eliminates tangles of wires.

OVERLEAF The iron pot rack, a collaborative design between blacksmith Frank Nowicki and designer Deena Perry, is conveniently hung over the center island.

OPPOSITE The height of the windows was determined in relation to seating positions, taking full advantage of the views outside. The table, by L. D. Burke, was hand painted, adzed, and edged with upholstery tacks. Beacon Indian blankets add a western flavor to the seating area.

ARCHITECT: ADRIAN AND LILA DEWINDT, DEWINDT AND ASSOCIATES, P.C.

INTERIOR DESIGNER: DEENA PERRY, HABITAT

CABINETS: WOOD DESIGN—ALASKAN CEDAR WITH "LIGHTNING" PATTERN AND PAINTED GLASS

COOKTOP: DACOR, SIX BURNERS

COUNTERTOP: AVONITE

DISHWASHER: THERMADOR

FLOOR: VERMONT SLATE

LIGHTING: HALO DOWNLIGHTS

OVEN: THERMADOR

POT RACK: IRONWOOD GALLERY, FRANK NOWICKI

REFRIGERATOR/FREEZER: SUB-ZERO

SINK: FRANKE

ABOVE The shades for the antler chandelier are punched, thickly painted linen.

BELOW Vintage leather postcards, found in an antique shop in Santa Fe, are used as coasters.

BELOW Of the home's six fireplaces, the shepherd's fireplace in the kitchen draws the most company. Shepherd's fireplaces were originally built in huts; steps led to a platform for sleeping.

Designed

.... *A selection of
kitchens that
resound with a
purity of line
and sense of
strategy*

Design Precision

· ·

When New York fashion executive Michael Abrams and his wife, Deborah, commissioned architect Scott Bromley to redesign their New York apartment, they were very definite about the plans for the kitchen. As Deborah remembers, "We started with the assumption that I would spend most of my life in the kitchen and so we asked ourselves, what would make me happy here?

"The first thing I wanted," said Deborah, "was a video setup so I could watch Julia Child while I was preparing food. I'd be able to put her on stop and just whip it up exactly the same way and start the tape again. I also wanted a great sound system in there—key tools to make me happy for hours."

Scott Bromley's initial step with the Abramses was to sit down with them and discuss what they were looking for in a kitchen. Dishwashers? They needed two. Sinks? They wanted two. Refrigerator? They chose a large industrial model with a wine cooler. Surfaces? They preferred stainless steel and granite.

To achieve the sleek, clean look that the owners sought, Bromley installed cabinets of bleached ash with black accents. The pulls are from Boffi, a Milan company, and the countertops are stainless steel, as is the backsplash. The counter on the island is a gray Lessinia stone.

Lighting was planned to accommodate the various uses of the kitchen from serious cooking to candlelight dinners. The lighting above the pot rack is halogen, as are the directional high hats in the ceiling. The architect feels that halogen "lets you see what you are doing

An unbroken line of stainless steel, as shown in the hood at left, accentuates the Gaggenau cooktop. At right, the laundry room has become part of the total kitchen design.

and also makes the food look great." The undercounter lights are incandescent.

An immovable column in the middle of the kitchen (which emerged out of an old kitchen and two maid's rooms) was encased in stainless steel and became the focal point for the island. With its NuTone control panel, the island is the soul of the kitchen, where the Abramses can do most of their prep work. Every inch counts—including the area above the cabinets, where the grillwork hides the speakers for the sound system. Even the microwave oven is tiny; it's used primarily for heating bagels, so, says Scott Bromley, "We got a bagel-sized microwave!"

OPPOSITE A large immovable column was encased in steel; it anchors the center island and also houses the sleek Kroin fixtures.

RIGHT A sliver cabinet next to the refrigerator becomes headquarters for baby paraphernalia.

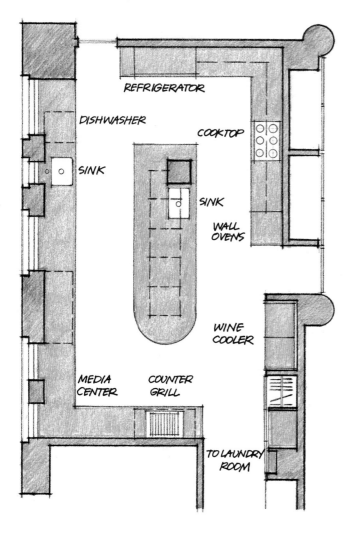

BELOW Equipment for playing everything from Julia Child on video to Harry Connick, Jr., on audio is encased in the recessed wall unit, keeping worktops free for kitchen tasks.

OVERLEAF The stainless steel is heat-resistant and hygienic; Lessinia stone from Italy is an elegant choice for the island.

ABOVE Canisters are set out on the counter. Accessories contribute to the design theme; everything from knife block to dish rack is black.

ABOVE Ingenious double-hinged, bi-fold doors eliminate wasted space in corner cupboards.

BELOW A variety of cutting boards.

BELOW Easy slide-out drawers were designed deep to accommodate a variety of equipment.

ABOVE Next to the wine cooler is an undersized Omni 5 oven. Recessed into the wall, it can microwave, microbake, toast, broil, and bake conventionally.

LEFT AND BELOW A Traulsen digital wine cooler is sleek and compact—a perfect choice for this sophisticated room. The wire racks are adjustable; the stainless-steel water bowls for the dogs are a touch of whimsy.

ARCHITECT: R. SCOTT BROMLEY
CABINETS AND PULLS: BOFFI, ITALY
COOKTOP: GAGGENAU
COUNTERTOP AND BACKSPLASH: STAINLESS STEEL
DISHWASHER: THERMADOR
FIXTURES: KROIN
FLOOR: BLEACHED AND TINTED OAK

GRILL: THERMADOR
ISLAND: LESSINIA STONE
LIGHTING: HALOGEN MR-16; INCANDESCENT UNDERCOUNTER
OVEN: GAGGENAU
REFRIGERATOR/FREEZER: TRAULSEN
SINK: ELKAY
WINE COOLER: TRAULSEN

A Worn Strategy

Designer Julie Atwood's challenge in this very formal San Francisco house was to create from scratch a kitchen that was elegant and "old world" in feeling, but that was also tough enough to stand up to the wear and tear of a heavy entertaining schedule. The owners wanted the kitchen to accommodate the needs of a professional caterer when big parties were on the agenda and yet not to overwhelm them when they prepared small dinners for family and friends.

Julie succeeded. The relatively small space is equipped with large-scale professional hardware, yet it is still cozy and warm.

The original kitchen—which featured wall-to-wall white steel cabinets (1930s vintage), accented by avocado appliances, and a floor of cracked linoleum—was totally gutted. Julie designed cabinets with three types of moldings—resulting in an "unfitted" look. These were finished with an ancient Chinese lacquer technique that achieved the "old and worn" finish she desired. Stainless-steel counters were chosen for their durability and look of an old-time scullery.

The butcher-block counter, which is set apart by being dropped a few inches, also functions as an impromptu desk, or a place to have a snack or breakfast for one. And the recycling unit, behind its formal cabinetry, is on castors, enabling it to be wheeled out to give the bartender and staff easy access for recycling. A nod to the rest of the house is the crown molding, which echoes the molding in the hall. Lighting is state of the art: industrial vapor-proof fixtures under the hood and low-voltage strip lighting under and above cabinets is smart and unobtrusive.

The deep red Chinese lacquer finish on unfitted custom cabinetry makes a rich and very individual statement in this small San Francisco kitchen.

ABOVE Cabinet doors open to reveal handsome fitted drawers for napkins, linens, and silver.

OPPOSITE A practical butcher-block slab runs between the two counters and does triple duty as menu planning area, chopping block, and breakfast nook.

RIGHT Bullnosed and painted in the same lacquer technique, the wood edging finishes the stainless-steel countertops, which was chosen by the designer for its durability and look of an old-time scullery.

BELOW Formerly used only in commercial kitchens, the open glass-fronted Traulsen refrigerator and freezer works surprisingly well in this small space.

ARCHITECT/INTERIOR DESIGNER: JULIE ATWOOD	**FIXTURE:** CHICAGO BLACK NICKEL
BUILDER: PARAGON GENERAL CONTRACTOR	**LIGHTING:** ANTIQUE HOLOPHANE INCANDESCENT; RECESSED HALOGEN
BACKSPLASH: BLACK AND GOLD MARBLE	**PULLS:** BALDWIN
CABINETS: ARTISAN WOOD WORKERS	**REFRIGERATOR:** TRAULSEN
COUNTERTOP: STAINLESS STEEL	**SINK:** KOHLER CAST-IRON IN JERSEY CREAM
DISHWASHER: HOBART	**STOVE:** VIKING
FLOOR: MAPLE STRIP WITH EBONIED BLACK WALNUT INLAY	**WALLS:** HAND-PAINTED BY CROWORKS

An Easy Fit

The Rees house on Long Island was originally designed in the late 1960s as a weekend residence for an active young family. In time, the family grew; the home became the family's main residence, and new needs required a new look. What was once a tiny kitchen was gutted and expanded by pushing out the back exterior walls. A large breakfast room open to the kitchen was added. Now this kitchen can handle any size crowd—which was a major goal of the owners.

The renovation was "a harmonious fit from beginning to end." Nan and Tom Rees both loved the colors and warmth of Sidona and Santa Fe (Tom grew up in the West) and wanted to bring that feeling to this room, so they chose their architect and builders with this in mind. All three men involved with the design and construction of the kitchen—the architect, David Stanton, and the contractors, Mark Gibson and Eric Schwenk —were educated in the West and shared their clients' love of the region's design aesthetic. "When we sat down with our architect and contractor we knew exactly what we wanted. We wanted to combine the strong design characteristics of New Mexico with the casual style of Long Island." The West also influenced many of the Reeses' choices of building materials, such as the Santillo Mexican tile that paves the floor and countertops, and the pine beams, handpicked by the contractor in New Hampshire.

Although rough-hewn and rustic, with its exposed beams and raised ceiling, the Reeses' kitchen also needed to work, especially for large gatherings, and that's when its ergonomics really shine. Nan Rees praises the "traffic pattern." During large parties, the center island's double butcher-block extensions come

The use of open beams and floating cabinets gives this Long Island kitchen an expansive southwestern look, while the choice of materials disguises its modern efficiency.

into play, extending the counter space and separating the cook from the crowd; they drop down when not in use. Double dishwashers also serve the Reeses well—as one fills up, the other is ready to go. And the commercial refrigerators and ovens are meant for the heavy-duty usage they get. "I wanted minimum repair and maximum service."

One ingenious touch is the dining table. Constructed out of cherry wood, it was faithfully copied by the African sculptor Jonathon Kenworthy from a table that the Reeses had dined at with friends in Kenya for many years. The entire center of the table works as a lazy Susan complete with a mesh of unseen gears underneath, and can completely revolve during meals. It is just one of the many objects picked up by Reeses in their travels that warms up the kitchen.

OPPOSITE Clever storage space abounds in this room, with drawers under the ovens and cabinets; high cupboards are for seldom-used items.

RIGHT Exposed beams above and Mexican tile below link the glass-enclosed breakfast room to the kitchen.

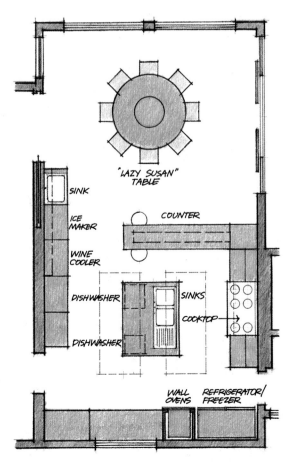

ARCHITECT: DAVID STANTON	ICEMAKER: WHIRLPOOL
CONTRACTORS: MARK GIBSON AND ERIC SCHWENK	LIGHTING: HALO AND LIGHTOLIER TRACK LIGHTING; LIGHTOLIER UNDER CABINET
CABINETS: CUSTOM BUILT, WHITE BIRCH	OVEN: THERMADOR PROFESSIONAL
COOKTOP: THERMADOR PROFESSIONAL	PULLS: AMEROCK
COUNTERTOP: SANTILLO MEXICAN TILE	REFRIGERATORS: TRAULSEN
DISHWASHERS: KITCHENAID	SINK: ELKAY
FIXTURES: AMEROCK	WALLS: SHEETROCK AND PAINT
FLOOR: SANTILLO MEXICAN TILE	WINE COOLER: JENN-AIR
FREEZER: TRAULSEN	

ABOVE Artifacts of a well-traveled family.

ABOVE The swinging door into the kitchen was fitted with a porthole.

OPPOSITE A large wooden and iron chandelier floats above the custom cherry lazy Susan kitchen table, helping to define an intimate dining area in this large open kitchen.

LEFT Double dishwashers and sinks, the expandable butcher-block worktop, and a large-size Traulsen refrigerator and freezer facilitate entertaining large groups.

An Authentic Sense

Andrée Putman's design sense was just the aesthetic that the owners of this apartment on Manhattan's Upper East Side had in mind when they began searching for the blueprint for their kitchen. "We spent a lot of time looking at different places and pictures in magazines and we always came back to this same style. And when we saw Morgan's Hotel in New York City we made the decision to work with Andrée," the world-renowned designer, noted for her furniture and interiors.

Although the rest of the apartment was reworked in a more classic Art Deco style, the kitchen remained true to the couple's dream. Both of them had always loved the well-designed look of diners and, combined with a "bit of nostalgia for our youth," they formulated their master plan—a highly sophisticated take on a diner—with Andrée and her New York associate, André Burgos, who oversaw the project together.

"After having made a list of the things we *had* to have, such as two sinks, a separate eating area, lots of light, counter space, and the glass brick wall, we sat down and talked specifics with our design team regarding such necessities as refrigerator, ovens, the dishwashers, and recycling. We ended up with just what we needed and more."

The L-shaped layout was simply a matter of available space. They knew they wanted to spend a lot of time here; they also wanted a large room and soon discovered the only way to expand the original kitchen and pantry was by moving the wall back three feet.

A collaboration between the design-conscious owners of this kitchen and designer Andrée Putman resulted in a crisp, slightly nostalgic room. The work area runs around two walls; intimate seating is opposite the curve.

The kitchen is filled with Putman design signatures. She pulled the cabinet handles out of a bag one day. "Andrée had just found them at a site that was being demolished," says the owner. Putman designed the kitchen table to work with the 1930 chairs by Robert Mallet Stevens. "The metal legs match the chair legs; the red and green Stop-and-Go levers and wheels were, again, Andrée's own brand of style."

But the owners took this kitchen a step further. Organized cooks, they found neat places for everything. Inveterate collectors, they used Bakelite and Depression glass and Fiesta Ware to imbue this very strong design space with their own personal statement.

LEFT An unobtrusive television set overlooks the black Formica table, designed by Andrée Putman, with Stop-and-Go levers and wheels at the base of its legs.

OPPOSITE Space limitations resulted in this handsome curved granite countertop. The quilted steel backsplash is a detail reminiscent of a Deco diner.

BELOW A decidedly architectural work space.

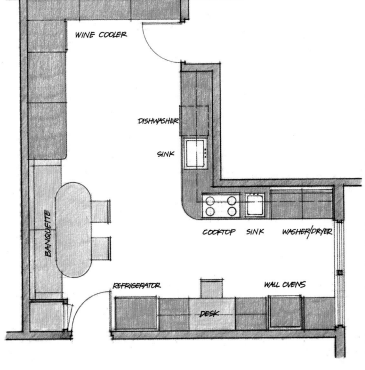

INTERIOR DESIGNER: ANDRÉE PUTMAN
CONTRACTOR: JOE LEONI OF LENNY
    CONSTRUCTION
PROJECT MANAGER: ANDRÉ BURGOS
BACKSPLASH: GRANITE; QUILTED
    STAINLESS STEEL; GLASS BLOCK
CABINETS: FORMICA
COOKTOP: CHAMBERS
COUNTERTOP: GRANITE
DISHWASHERS: KITCHENAID AND ROPER
FIXTURES: CHICAGO
FLOOR: CERAMIC TILE
LIGHTING: HIGH HATS; ARTEMIDE
    CEILING FIXTURE; UNDERCOUNTER
    FLUORESCENT
OVEN: THERMADOR
PULLS: SALVAGED CAST ALUMINUM FROM
    THE FIFTIES
REFRIGERATOR/FREEZER: SUB-ZERO
SINKS: ELKAY

LEFT Fold-out pantry doors expand storage capabilities.

BELOW LEFT Knives and utensils are stored beneath the Chambers cooktop.

OPPOSITE The granite backsplash and the Chicago faucet complement the room's architectural feel; the cruet bottle used as detergent container adds a small personal touch.

OVERLEAF At left, Formica cabinets were custom built above and below to match the curve of the granite. At right, the owners were able to install the glass brick wall they had always wanted by pushing a wall back three feet into the adjoining room.

Drama at Hand

Although it suggests the perfect summer place, with its spacious high ceilings and unobstructed views of the Atlantic, the Della Femina weekend kitchen, highlighted by its center island built-in grill, works extraordinarily well year-round.

One decidedly dramatic design decision was to increase the height of the kitchen ceiling to sixteen feet. This created an illusion of more space—an important ingredient for Jerry, who likes to gather his friends in the kitchen while he cooks. Jerry and his newscaster wife, Judy Licht, also removed a tiny casement window, adding a wall of glass instead and hung pots and pans from the ceiling to soften the architectural lines of the kitchen. Because this was a relatively small space to begin with, each element was designed to function as efficiently as possible.

The pièce de résistance, in the eyes of Della Femina, is the working island, which he rhapsodizes as "this giant structure in the middle of the room with its own sink, grill, recycling center and, best of all, a view." This work core is constructed in such a way that he can reach for just about anything, from the spices to the spigot without having to nudge a guest or ask for assistance. Its butcher-block top creates an instant chopping board.

Kitchen philosopher Della Femina has a theory: "What starts out as a luxury inevitably turns out to be a necessity—especially so in the case of the spigot jutting out from the Garland stove." It, he discovered, eliminates the need for lifting heavy pots of water from the sink to the stove for lobster and pasta—and pasta is on the menu at least once every weekend.

At left, a custom-designed pot rack dramatizes the sixteen-foot-high ceiling of the rather small, squarish room. At right, a spice drawer—angled for easy access—is conveniently next to the stove and beneath the granite countertop.

ARCHITECT: FRANK HOLLENBECK
BUILDER: BEN KRUPINSKI
INTERIOR DESIGNER: LAWRENCE PEABODY
CABINETS: HENSLER AND WHITNEY
  WOODWORK
COUNTERTOP: GRANITE
DISHWASHER: KITCHENAID
FIXTURES: CHICAGO
FLOOR: MEXICAN TILE
GRILL: JENN-AIR
LIGHTING: ALCO, SKYLIGHT: VELUX
POT RACK: CUSTOM DESIGNED
PULLS: BALDWIN BRASS
REFRIGERATOR/FREEZER: SUB-ZERO
SINK: ELKAY
STOVE: GARLAND

BELOW Della Femina, known as well for his culinary expertise as for his advertising genius, cleans the catch of the day. The handy Chicago faucet makes light work of numerous kitchen chores such as this one.

OPPOSITE A wall of glass was created to capture the view of the Atlantic Ocean. A Jenn-Air grill is built right into the butcher-block island.

ABOVE An ingenious stovetop spigot helps facilitate countless pasta and seafood dinners.

Spare

.... *Six
kitchens
that elevate
understatement
to an art*

Deliberate Restraint

Karin Blake's kitchen on Martha's Vineyard is as simple and straightforward as her approach to design. "I've always wanted to restore an old house," she has said. As a child growing up near a Quaker community in Bucks County, Pennsylvania, Karin was influenced by the clean, uncluttered look of her surroundings. Summering on Cape Cod—where her grandmother had an extensive collection of antiques—she developed an abiding interest in and a passion for early American furniture and objects.

The farmhouse she bought on Martha's Vineyard had remained within one family for more than two hundred years, but additions had been made over time. Much of its original charm was hidden under years of renovation and redecoration. Karin's approach was to remove rather than add, and her kitchen best shows off this technique.

It's her favorite room because "that's where families come together. You may not go into your living room for weeks, but the kitchen is where everybody meets in the morning and usually just before going to bed."

Originally two small, dark rooms, the space was taken down to its bare bones. Karin exposed the original sheathing and framing and made one large, open space out of the two rooms. To add much-needed light, she put a pair of French doors in one wall, but she eliminated as many "unnecessary" doors as she could.

Karin uses the house primarily in the summer. Uncomplicated entertaining is the order of the day, so she had little need or want for the latest in kitchen equip-

This kitchen was restored by paring down rather than adding on. The rustic feel of the old farm table and mixed chairs in this light-filled summer room makes it a natural gathering spot for family and friends.

ment. She has kept everything deliberately restrained and simple with only a sturdy stove, dishwasher, and refrigerator.

Perhaps most interesting is the old soapstone sink. Original to the kitchen, it was covered in a thick black paint which Karin labored over and removed during renovation. Now it anchors one wall—along with an old plate rack.

The room serves as a tempered backdrop for the sturdy lines of the American pieces—the old farm table and mixed chairs, for example—that are the signature of this designer. The floors are painted with basic floor paint which gradually wears down and creates a very natural look. "I put a new coat of paint on it every two years—the way the farmers always did."

For the owner, the room evokes poignant feelings. "The smell of wax, mixed with the old, musty smell when you open a cupboard is so familiar to me—it's a strong childhood memory."

Haunted House 693-6956
Julie
PAUL Silva 645-2251
PeTer 0935
693-6541
Eve Stone 693-0296
X Mrs Marlow 805 563-0867
RUBIN
Mark 6931390
Leslie 6982696

homeport 645-2679
OysterBar 693-3300

SARAh 645-9106

Nathan 6934110

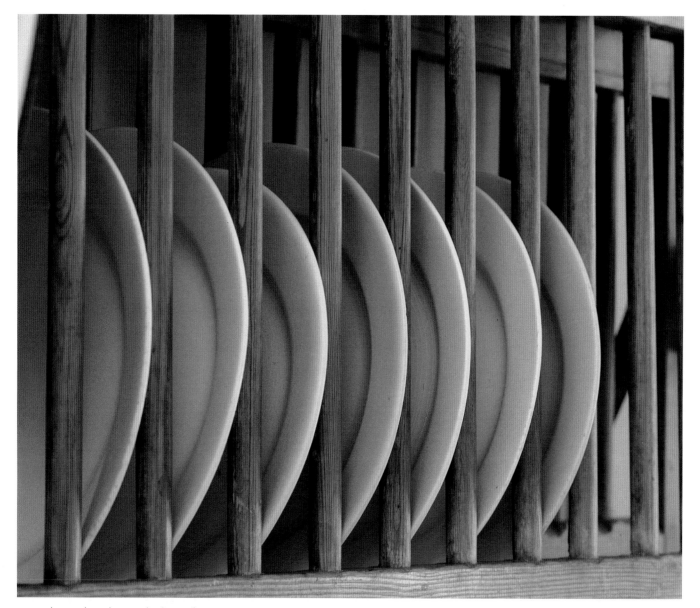

ABOVE A wooden plate rack above the soapstone sink serves dual purposes: It facilitates dish drying, and it creates an aesthetically pleasing break on a wall where a window was not logistically possible.

RIGHT Rain gear and a barn-door bell hang from a pegged coat rack right off the dining room.

OPPOSITE An old soapstone sink was stripped down and moved from one side of the room to the other, and an extra-long commercial faucet was installed. The Martha's Vineyard clam basket is filled with quahogs; local Queen Anne's lace sits in a blue-sponge tin bucket.

DESIGNER: KARIN BLAKE
BUILDER: PETER MARZBANIAN
ANTIQUES: RICHARD MULLIGAN; EVE
  STONE & SON
COUNTERTOP: MAPLE BUTCHER BLOCK
DISHWASHER: KENMORE
FAN: MIAMI/CAREY EXHAUST FAN
FIXTURES: COMMERCIAL
FLOOR: PAINTED WOODEN FLOORS
LIGHTING: IRON CHANDELIER; RECESSED
  HIGH HATS
REFRIGERATOR/FREEZER: KENMORE
STOVE: U.S. RANGE

A Kitchen Discovered

Detlef and Anna Pump moved to the farm-house in Sag Harbor because on their first visit to this old whaling community on the eastern end of Long Island, "the air smelled the same, the land felt the same" as the small village in their native Germany that they had left more than thirty years earlier. In other words, it was like home. But they realized a massive renovation was required. The house had been turned into three separate apartments with as many kitchens.

While examining the basement (often the best way to figure out the original layout of an old home), Detlef found not only the old kitchen, but also the remarkable beehive fireplace.

Detlef's and Anna's careers and professional interests—he is a successful builder and she is an accomplished cookbook author, caterer, and co-owner of Loaves and Fishes, a gourmet shop in Bridgehampton —combined to create a plethora of knowledge about kitchens. They collaborated in producing a room that satisfied Detlef's prediliction for the ergonomics of kitchen planning along with Anna's requirements for the more practical aspects of cooking.

Much of the original exterior pine planks were recycled by Detlef for the cabinet fronts, the free-standing pantry, even the ceilings. The island, topped with granite, neatly divides the work area from the dining area; it also does double duty as a bar when the Pumps entertain in the kitchen. Commercial additions like the U.S. Range coexist with the beehive oven. It all adds up to a workable space with primitive undertones.

At right, a worn Oriental runner offers a strong counterpoint to the industrial lines of a U.S. Range. The 150-year-old beams were exposed; industrial steel runners and meat hooks were attached (see left and right), creating overhead pot storage.

ABOVE The old beehive fireplace is located to the left of the work island. Restored, it and its pottery-covered mantel serve as the room's focal point.

BELOW The open layout is deceptively simple; Detlef's knowledge of ergonomics has made it eminently practical.

ABOVE Comfortable mismatched chairs and an antique walnut table stand in as a "kitchen set" in front of the fireplace.

BUILDER AND DESIGNER: DETLEF PUMP
BACKSPLASH: NEW PINE, PAINTED WHITE
CABINETS: ORIGINAL EXTERIOR PINE
   PLANKS RECYCLED
COOKTOP: U.S. RANGE
COUNTERTOP: GRANITE
DISHWASHER: KITCHENAID
FIXTURES: AMERICAN STANDARD
FLOOR: ORIGINAL PINE BOARDS
LIGHTING: SURFACE-MOUNTED SPOT
   LIGHTING
OVEN: U.S. RANGE
POT RACK: IRON DESIGNED BY DETLEF
   PUMP
PULLS: WOODEN
REFRIGERATOR/FREEZER: GENERAL
   ELECTRIC
SINK: STAINLESS-STEEL AMERICAN
   STANDARD
WALLS: PLASTER-OVER-PLASTER LATH,
   AND PLANKING UP TO CHAIR RAIL

ABOVE Gray speckled granite is used on the counter as well as on the island.

RIGHT The free-standing pantry was created out of original pine planks left over from the renovation.

OVERLEAF The original windows had to be raised to accommodate the height of the granite counter. Detlef added two more windows at the same time.

Barn Redux

In the early 1980s, Raymond and Mariette Gomez bought three dairy barns clustered together on Long Island. These individual structures became one house, as Raymond, an architect with Edward Durell Stone Associates, succeeded in connecting the barns without moving them.

"Raymond really laid out the plans and figured out exactly how the flow would work," explains Mariette, an interior designer. "We both agreed we wanted the children's section on one side, our bedroom and guest bedrooms on the other, and the public spaces—the living room and the kitchen—right in the middle."

There were two absolutes in the Gomez kitchen plans. First, the kitchen had to be in the rear of the house, with windows to take advantage of the interesting play of sunlight and a back door to give them full access to the outdoor space, especially in the summer. Second, it had to be large. After all, this was a weekend house built for family and entertaining.

The Gomezes put the architectural idiosyncrasy of their dairy barns to imaginative use. They left three stall rooms intact in the kitchen. One became the laundry room; the second, Raymond's tool room and workroom; the third, Mariette's potting shed. The space between the work and the stall areas was deliberately kept open, with an old kitchen table, found in New Hampshire, as the focal point.

The open plan works well in the Gomez house. When the children were younger, the kitchen was the room where all would congregate and now, whether the family is together or entertaining friends, it still works as a space where everyone can gather, assuring that the cook will never be left isolated.

Four eighteenth-century French lithographs, which the owner has had for years, peer out from the open cupboards over a triple sink by Elkay.

ABOVE The black granite is a stylish counterpoint to the original barn siding. The white dishes are from Wolfman Gold & Good Company in New York City.

The work area is anchored by the L-shaped island highlighted by a Jenn-Air indoor grill, which is vented under the counter toward the sink to the exterior wall.

Open shelves were Mariette's idea; placing them directly over the sink and dishwasher area allows easy access for unloading the machine. Stylish black granite counters, which blend with the rich pine cabinets, were chosen for a more practical purpose—pastry making by mother and daughter.

In addition to high hats that wash the front of the cabinets, imaginative lighting effects were achieved by the use of Artemide's halogen light—one similar to those used on bridges—which was affixed to the ceiling beams, succeeding in giving the Gomezes the requisite lighting for the work area.

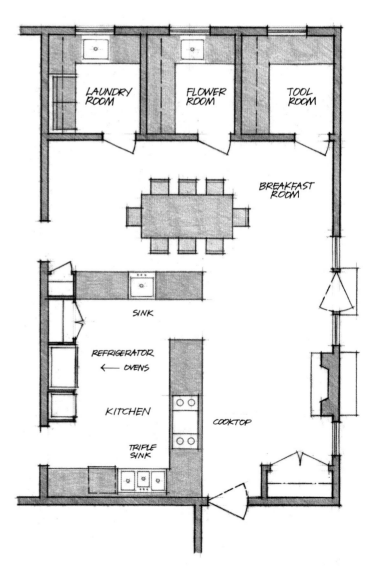

ABOVE At the far end of the kitchen, three stalls from the original barn have been transformed into a potting shed, a laundry room, and a tool room.

BELOW LEFT Framed with ivy, the kitchen door leads to the pool and gardens. The rustic twig rocker is from the Adirondacks.

BELOW RIGHT The open shelves contribute a sense of ease to the kitchen area. Spoons and utensils are stored in old crocks and buckets.

ABOVE The painted wood cupboard—purchased many years ago in New Hampshire—is used to store glassware. A second sink is conveniently located for use when entertaining guests.

OPPOSITE Old wire baskets add a sense of geometry to the pine mantel.

RIGHT The new white pine floor was specially stained to look old.

ARCHITECT: RAYMOND GOMEZ OF
    EDWARD DURELL STONE ASSOCIATES
INTERIOR DESIGNER: MARIETTE HIMES
    GOMEZ
CABINETS: SHAKER-DESIGNED FLAT
    PANEL PINE FABRICATED BY WOODY
    MOSCH
COOKTOP: JENN-AIR
COUNTERTOP: ANDES BLACK GRANITE
DISHWASHER: KITCHENAID
FIXTURES: ELKAY
FLOOR: PINE PLANK
GRILL: JENN-AIR
LIGHTING: ARTEMIDE HALOGEN;
    DAYLIGHT FLUORESCENT;
    INCANDESCENT DOWN LIGHT
OVEN: JENN-AIR
PULLS: SHAKER, FABRICATED BY
    WOODY MOSCH
REFRIGERATOR/FREEZER: GENERAL
    ELECTRIC
SINK: ELKAY

Understated Chic

Gennifer Witbeck's handsome kitchen reflects the diverse talents and interests she brings to her career as an interior designer for a select list of clients. Pointing to her particular sense of style are the bistro chairs from Les Galeries Lafayette in Paris, the sink fixture from an industrial restaurant supply store in lower Manhattan, and the antique chandelier rescued from a junkyard.

Gennifer's weekend house is a charming cottage in a Long Island seaside town. Most first-time visitors think the old kitchen has just been updated a bit and are surprised to learn it was completely gutted.

The aesthetic focal point in the kitchen is undoubtedly the hand-painted black-and-white checkerboard floor, inspired, says Gennifer, by a "Vermeer painting that featured a central stove, a seventeenth-century chandelier, and a black-and-white tile floor." The floor complements the kitchen's industrial hardware and Old World glass cabinetry.

To keep the "pantry look" that she wanted, Gennifer decided not to put in a tall refrigerator. Rather, she devised a small center work island with an under-the-counter refrigerator. Wainscoting adds character. And among the many clever innovations is the banquette seating that doubles as storage.

Efficiency was the key to this small yet elegant kitchen. A wooden banquette with storage underneath runs the length of one wall, ending in an intimate dining area.

ABOVE The banquette with multicolored Indian silk pillows is an inviting corner for visiting friends.

OPPOSITE Black Calphalon pots hang from a brass runner. The small center island holds the kitchen's little refrigerator; the racks keep towels and oven mitts handy.

BELOW The double sink has an industrial faucet with a separate spray from New York's Bowery Restaurant Supply.

ABOVE The banquette opens to provide extra storage space for party supplies.

INTERIOR DESIGNER: GENNIFER (VIRGINIA) WITBECK

CABINETS: CUSTOM-BUILT WITH EGGSHELL FINISH

COOKTOP: GAGGENAU

COUNTERTOP: TWO-INCH MAPLE BUTCHER BLOCK

DISHWASHER: KITCHENAID

FIXTURES: BOWERY RESTAURANT SUPPLY

FLOOR: CUSTOM-PAINTED BY BOBBI JONES

LIGHTING: ANTIQUE CHANDELIER

OVEN: GAGGENAU

POT RACK: CUSTOM DESIGN

PULLS: REPRODUCTION KNOBS, KRAFT HARDWARE

REFRIGERATOR/FREEZER: SUB-ZERO UNDERCOUNTER

SINK: ELKAY STAINLESS STEEL

WALLS: SEMI-GLOSS PAINT OVER EXISTING WAINSCOT WALLS

A Light Transformation

No structural changes were required when Karin Blake and William Levine set about to renovate the kitchen of their Malibu countryside home. A series of quick cosmetic changes in the kitchen achieved the desired effect. "We whitened the entire room—lightening all the wood and bleaching the dark wood floors," says Karin.

Karin then altered the bookcase in the breakfast area to accommodate her collection of birdhouses and firkins—small wooden vessels that she has accumulated over the years. "I love all the old things that go in a kitchen," she says. "The ancient tables and chairs and tools . . . I'm always on the prowl looking for them." They now form the backdrop, along with some of her other, equally colorful, early American pieces, for the eating and work areas of the kitchen.

The double island also gets high ratings from its owners. It was already in place when they moved in, but Karin, an interior designer, has adapted this convenient idea for many of her clients. "You turn around from the triple sink to the butcher-block island to chop —and you're right there." Underneath one of the islands is a waste area, divided into sections for recycling, while the other island holds storage space for oversized pots and pans. And rather than continue the wood on the floor, they have ceramic tile between the two islands, to expedite clean-up and maintenance.

Here some simple cosmetic changes and a few well-thought-out additions produced the clean, pure kitchen that the Levines sought.

At left, a cat sits comfortably atop a Wolf stove. At right, an American cupboard with its original paint, circa 1850, houses Karin's "Asiatic Pheasant" Staffordshire.

INTERIOR DESIGNER: KARIN BLAKE
ANTIQUES: RICHARD MULLIGAN
CABINETS: PAINTED WOOD
COUNTERTOP: BUTCHER BLOCK
DISHWASHER: KITCHENAID
FLOOR: WOOD AND CERAMIC TILE
LIGHTING: CUSTOM CHROME
REFRIGERATOR/FREEZER: SUB-ZERO
STOVE: WOLF
SINK: ELKAY

LEFT A six-burner Wolf stove with griddle is recessed into the wall adjacent to the two work islands.

BELOW A triple stainless-steel sink, equipped with a single faucet, a hot water dispenser, and a retractable spray hose, eases chores.

BELOW The lighting unit was designed to correspond to the double island. Having two islands puts everything within easy reach of the cook. The wooden floors of the kitchen and dining area have been bleached.

ABOVE Simple recessed shelves hold a collection of baskets, firkins, and birdhouses, forming a backdrop for the breakfast room.

RIGHT The overblown roses on the dining table are from Karin's garden.

BELOW A simple painted box holds tennis equipment in a corner by the back door.

The Heart of the Home

Leslie King grew up in a house where the kitchen was the center of all activity and she wanted the same for her own kitchen. There is no center island here but, rather, a kitchen table that is used for everything from meal planning and preparation to homework and visiting and, of course, dining.

King and her designer, Karin Blake, originally envisioned adding space by knocking down the wall between the kitchen and butler's pantry—since this was an arrangement designed for a staff and not a family with three active boys. But eventually they decided to keep the pantry for "its architectural integrity." Needed space came from a maid's back room, which provided them with an additional pantry, or larder, behind the kitchen table.

"That little pantry not only holds foodstuffs but also crayons, paintbrushes, art supplies, sports equipment —each in a separate wire basket," Leslie says. "Every child who walks into our house gets to know that pantry intimately."

Because Leslie collects American primitive pieces, she wanted to keep her kitchen "plain and simple." The new off-white board and batten cabinets with reproduction Shaker knobs have clean lines. And the pumpkin and off-white stenciled floor was hand-painted to be the anchor of the room. But the gem of this kitchen is the original O'Keefe and Merritt stove (one of only eight hundred made). It was rechromed and relined, but the porcelain was left as is to avoid a brand-new look.

This classic butler's pantry was preserved in its original state. The antique secretary at the far end is used by Leslie for menu planning and list writing.

INTERIOR DESIGNER: KARIN BLAKE
CABINETS: BOARD AND BATTEN
COUNTERTOP: BUTCHER BLOCK
DISHWASHER: KITCHENAID ENERGY
    SAVER
FIXTURE: CHICAGO
FLOOR: WIDE-PLANKED, STENCILED
LIGHTING: RECESSED LIGHTING;
    ANTIQUE CHANDELIER FROM
    RICHARD MULLIGAN
PULLS: REPRODUCTION SHAKER
REFRIGERATOR/FREEZER: SUB-ZERO
SINK: ELKAY
STOVE: O'KEEFE AND MERRITT
TABLE: SHAKER-STYLE

LEFT The decorator designed a new stainless-steel hood to complement the restored O'Keefe and Merritt stove. The wide-planked floor was painted on the diagonal to increase the width of the room visually.

BELOW Wooden shelving is used for the larder, along with wire pull-out baskets.

ABOVE Antique hickory chairs surround the multipurpose early American kitchen table; an iron chandelier hangs above it. The narrow door leading to the pantry was salvaged from a 1940s farmhouse.

LEFT The bottom three drawers are cleverly concealed behind a board-and-batten cabinet door panel.

RIGHT The corner cabinet is outfitted with lazy Susan shelves, taking full advantage of the space.

Personal

.... *Seven kitchens*
that bear
the stamp of
individual style

Foggy Illusions

Agnes Bourne and Jim Leubbers live on one of the highest floors in a classical, older co-op building in San Francisco. "We wanted to feel as if we were living in the clouds," says Agnes. So they decided to try to capture that feeling. Agnes, a designer of interiors and furniture, worked with painter Shelly Masters to create this misty illusion. Mythical icons, symbols, and trompe l'oeil designs float over a gray-mist background and add up to atmosphere with a message. The eye on the hood over the stove, for example, symbolizes that Jim, an ophthamologist who also does all the cooking, is high priest of this temple.

Agnes was determined to preserve as much as she could of the original 1926 kitchen design. The trash disposal chute, the bell indicator and intercom, and the fold-out ironing board were all in perfect working order, and they remain. But she did make changes.

Three feet of wall space stolen from the old pantry create an open area that Agnes zoned into three sections, for prep, clean up, and dining. The prep area consists of granite countertops with a mirrored backsplash. The clean-up area, separated by a partially mirrored partition, has an extra deep sink, a dishwasher, and an undercounter Sub-Zero freezer. The demi-lune marble slab, used for buffets and small meals, was inspired by the Italian trattorias that Agnes and Jim love. She designed the countertop so it is just large enough to completely unfold the morning paper with one's breakfast. In keeping with the owners' preservation tenets, the floors are simply the original linoleum painted over with deck paint.

At left, in a whimsical salute to one of its owners—an ophthamologist—a trompe l'oeil eye presides over the Viking stove with mirrored backsplash. At right, some of the apartment's original workings—the doorbell and intercom, for example—stand out against the hand-painted walls.

ABOVE Ingenious storage space abounds in unusual places. All of it was created by the owner, a furniture designer and interior decorator.

ABOVE Another remnant from the twenties—the garbage hopper—stands out from the mirrored backsplash.

OPPOSITE Four unglazed ceramic vessels crown the hand-rubbed ash cabinetry. Jeff Benedetto's creative chopping-block table, with its "high power line" legs, is in the foreground.

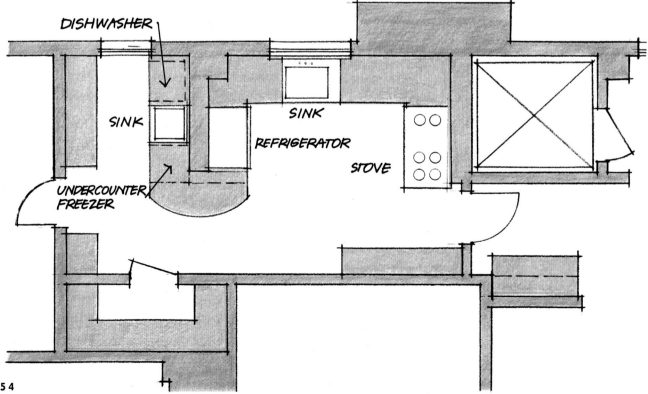

DISHWASHER

SINK

SINK

REFRIGERATOR

STOVE

UNDERCOUNTER FREEZER

ARCHITECT: AGNES BOURNE, INC.

INTERIOR AND PRODUCT DESIGNER: AGNES
BOURNE

CABINET: CABINET WORKS STAINED ASH

CHOPPING-BLOCK TABLE: JEFF BENEDETTO

COUNTERTOPS: IMPERIAL BLUE GRANITE;
CARRERRA MARBLE

DISHWASHER: ASSEA (SWEDISH-MADE)

FIXTURES: KWC

FLOOR: PAINTED LINOLEUM

FREEZER: SUB-ZERO UNDERCOUNTER

LIGHTING: HALO RECESSED LIGHTING;
"ARETUSA" HANGING FIXTURE BY
ARTIMEDE

PULLS: MERIT PULLS; BALDWIN KNOBS

REFRIGERATOR: SUB-ZERO

SINKS: FRANKE

STOVE: VIKING

VENETIAN BLINDS: NANICK TWO-INCH
WOODEN BLINDS

WALLS: CUSTOM PAINTED BY SHELLEY
MASTERS

OPPOSITE A striking Japanese kitchen
shrine is stationed above the cleanup
area; newspapers are stored in the
circular cutouts. Wooden blinds were
chosen to direct the sometimes intense
light in this penthouse apartment.

RIGHT Carrerra marble is used on the
trattoria-like breakfast nook; a trompe
l'oeil pediment surrounds the doorway.

Flea Market Fancy

Arnelle Kase has always had a penchant for rescuing things deemed ugly by others. It began when she was five years old and would trail her mother to rummage sales at their local church. Some of her "prized orphans," as Arnelle calls them, formulate the statement made by her kitchen in the heart of San Francisco. "The kitchen was primarily designed to function for dinner parties large and small, but it had to be a backdrop for my many collections as well."

She also wanted a space that had a comfortable fit with the rest of the primarily Edwardian house. "The architecture of the house is on the serious side, but I didn't want to continue that strictness into the kitchen." So by parodying the columns in the front hall with a pair of more whimsical ones in the back of the kitchen, Arnelle began to set a lighter tone.

A former caterer, she knew the prerequisites for a workable kitchen and decided that a long galley with a raised seating area at one end made great sense. The fact that the plumbing was already in place along one wall helped influence her decision to keep these elements to one side.

The old Irish pine island, found on another weekend foray, helped define the work space and partially separate the cook from company; at the same time, it added much-needed storage for oversized pieces. All other cabinets below waist level are equipped with either a drawer or a shelf that pulls out, so no space is "lost" in the back; this is a feature that Arnelle and the design firm she works for, Barbara Scavullo Associates, include in all their kitchen projects.

The handsome Irish pine island creates easy and accessible storage and work space in this long, galley-style kitchen.

ABOVE One of the secrets to this well-organized kitchen is the storage: cabinet doors conceal a variety of pull-outs; one of the deep drawers was designed to accommodate a hanging file for recipes.

LEFT Hand-painted tiles from "Dish-is-it" are interspersed on the backsplash with a plain and speckled pattern. Among the owner's collectibles on display are a vintage toaster and cow creamer.

INTERIOR DESIGNER: ARNELLE KASE
CONTRACTOR: PLATH AND COMPANY
BACKSPLASH: DISH-IS-IT'S HAND-PAINTED TILE
CABINETS: CUSTOM-DESIGNED BY ARNELLE KASE
COUNTERTOP: COLORCORE PLASTIC LAMINATE
DISHWASHER: KITCHENAID
FIXTURES: DELTA
FLOOR: VPI'S "TERRALAST"
LIGHTING: TRONCONI'S "SOLITAIRE"
PULLS: FORMS AND SURFACES' FORMED NEOPRENE
REFRIGERATOR/FREEZER: GENERAL ELECTRIC
SINK: FRANKE
STOVE: U.S. RANGE
WASHER/DRYER: WESTINGHOUSE

RIGHT The stacked washer and dryer are concealed behind a pair of doors.

BELOW The owner bumped out this end of the room, adding glass doors for light and columns for whimsy. She further separated the dining area by raising the floor a few inches. The chairs are a flea-market find; the table, her own design.

BELOW Compartments within drawers provide organized storage space for an avid baker.

Bringing the Country to Town

In a city where living space is notoriously limited, the Park Avenue apartment of Friederike and Jeremy Biggs offers the luxury of living on three generously sized floors graced by terraces and a roof garden. Consequently, their kitchen is a large one by New York City standards—"It's our country house and city house rolled into one," says Friederike—and it allows them design and decorating opportunities not usually found in city apartments.

The couple's kitchen renovation was primarily cosmetic, with minimal structural changes. Aging white floor tiles were removed and replaced with Genuwood, an inexpensive vinyl flooring that resembles wood (using a thicker tile would have meant ripping out all the cabinets to accommodate it). Cabinets and walls were simply painted off-white and then combed over with a honey-colored glaze. "We cut some 'teeth' into a rubber squeegee and used it for the plaid effect," says Friederike.

Storage space abounds in odd, out-of-the-way places in the kitchen. Friederike now has a separate desk area to coordinate menus and schedules; she was able to remove a table and telephone that were under the stairs and add a much-needed second refrigerator—"a great utilization of a funny space." A trompe l'oeil door —an oenophile's fantasy—was painted on the refrigerator panel by Christian Brandner.

Since Friederike loves to cook, she chose a Traulsen refrigerator and a large commercial Garland stove with

At one end of the room is banquette seating covered in a practical, vinylized Brunschwig & Fils fabric; around the old pine trestle table are black Regency chairs with cushions to match the banquette. The Hermann M. Biggs of the "clean plate" poster at right is a former commissioner of the New York State Department of Health—and Jeremy's uncle.

ABOVE An antique pine box is used to store cocktail napkins.

BELOW Decked out with some of the owner's extensive collection of cooking utensils and topped with her design signature—birdcages—is the six-burner, two-oven Garland range. Pale blue-and-white tiles surround the stove, making for easy cleanup and keeping the appliance from overwhelming the space.

six burners and a double oven with a griddle. "I did put the stove on an electric pilot light, though, since gas does generate a lot of heat."

Friederike loves antiques and uses them wherever she can. Witness the Regency chairs, the old pine trestle table, and her china collection. She also cleverly camouflaged all the old pipes and valves that must be accessible in city apartments by placing antique birdcages, one of her design signatures, over them throughout the kitchen; they lend a whimsical aviary touch to the room. Her practical side, however, will prevail if she feels the antiques won't be functional. With a careful selection of details, the Biggses have created a city kitchen with a decidedly country look.

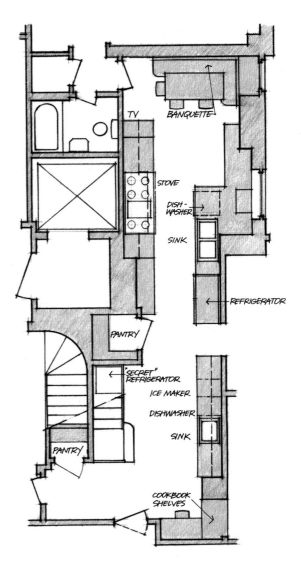

OPPOSITE A birdcage, a cricket cage, a painted coffeepot, and pineapples (a symbol of hospitality) personalize this corner.

ABOVE Friederike's design touches link the kitchen to the rest of the house. This Regency-style black-and-gold birdcage is in the dining room.

RIGHT Hand-painted butterscotch walls and bleached wooden countertops frame a window of topiaries resting on a self-draining, pebble-based sill.

BELOW A baker's trio: three deep drawers are reserved for measuring cups, jars, and flour.

ABOVE AND RIGHT Christian Brandner's trompe l'oeil under the stairs, a wine lover's fantasy, conceals a necessary second refrigerator and a vertical slice of cabinet shelving.

OPPOSITE The owner kept the original hand-painted door that leads to the dining room and used it to determine the color palette for the kitchen.

INTERIOR DESIGNER: FRIEDERIKE KEMP
   BIGGS OF KEMP INTERIORS, INC.
CABINETS: CUSTOM PAINTED BY FRED
   HOBERLE
COUNTERTOP: BLEACHED TEAK
DISHWASHER: KITCHENAID
FIXTURES: KWC
FLOOR: GENUWOOD BY PERMAGRAIN
   PRODUCTS, INC.
LIGHTING: LIGHTOLIER
REFRIGERATORS: TRAULSEN,
   WESTINGHOUSE
SINK: ELKAY
STOVE: GARLAND, SIX-BURNER, DOUBLE
   OVEN
TROMPE L'OEIL ARTIST: CHRISTIAN
   BRANDNER
WALLS: CUSTOM PAINTED BY FRED
   HOBERLE

New England Honesty

Visitors to Alan Campbell's kitchen end up sharing feelings of nostalgia. This 150-year-old Connecticut kitchen is pure of spirit, with its clean blue and white lines and its original sink still intact. Yet everything—walls, ceiling, floor—was totally taken apart and put back together. New appliances were added, and an old closed pantry was subtracted.

In place of the pantry Alan put a table, chairs, a low cabinet, and some of the original shelves of the former pantry, creating his own open shelving. He also left the double sink as a second sink, handy for washing oversized pots and platters and for arranging flowers and repotting plants.

Behind the kitchen door is more open shelving—all new. Across from it is an old white enamel-and-wood table that was found in the house and is a great catch-all space. The J.D. Brauner center island worktable is not that unusual, but Alan points out that it is "the best, with the work space on top and the storage space underneath."

Because Alan is a fabric designer—he designs for Alan Campbell Fabrics and Wallcoverings of China Seas—he was immediately attracted to the original blue in the kitchen, and he repainted in the same colorway. He also decided to keep his classic pieces—the round Saarinen table from Knoll International, and Prague chairs from Stendig—which have been with him for years, survivors of his "International Style" period and now perfectly at home in his charming Greek Revival home.

The original blue color, dating back a hundred years, is the pervasive theme in the kitchen. Repetition is also a key, with collections of colanders and pitchers simply and honestly displayed.

OPPOSITE AND RIGHT Shelves from the original pantry were used to create open shelf space in this corner. A part of two shelves was reserved for Alan's collection of white Wedgwood china.

ABOVE Painted wood cabinets frame one end of the kitchen. The shelves are narrow, but it's easy to spot what you're looking for when they're only one jar deep.

RIGHT Brauner's classic butcher-block table works equally well for chores and snacks.

INTERIOR DESIGNER: ALAN CAMPBELL
CHAIRS: STENDIG'S PRAGUE
COUNTERTOP: FORMICA
DISHWASHER: IN-SINK-ERATOR
FLOOR: KENTILE
REFRIGERATOR: KELVINATOR
STOVE: WHIRLPOOL
TABLE: KNOLL'S SAARINEN

Nostalgia with a Twist

When it came to laying out and planning her own southern California kitchen, Kitty Bartholomew was able to bring to bear her expertise as the decorator for ABC's *Home* show. Kitty had kept clipping files on kitchens she had seen over the years and knew she loved the charm and informality of old-fashioned ones. After analyzing her needs, she knocked down the walls of three rooms and dug in.

Kitty added chicken-wire glass inserts to one of the cabinet fronts to make it look more like an old-fashioned cupboard. Vintage potholders and pots, salt and pepper shakers, bird cages, and a vast collection of red-and-white utensils from the thirties, the results of Kitty's avid treasure hunting throughout Maine, support the kitchen's old-fashioned theme. Dramatic and extensive use of black and white tiles adds to the eclectic mood.

Her pièce de résistance is a striking 1947 O'Keefe and Merritt Town & Country stove on permanent loan from a friend. Restored and refurbished to its former glory, it's ideal for baking bread and stews in the Bartholomew household.

To complement the nostalgic feeling that the stove created, Kitty was inspired to design a refrigerator that would have the feel of an old icebox but would function as well as a state-of-the-art model. She worked with a local commercial refrigerator company (found in the Yellow Pages), and put doors on both sides for easy access. Also ingenious are the baskets Kitty uses to group foods.

Backsplash panels of painted barnyard scenes soften the look of the custom-built undercounter glass refrigerator. The extensive use of glass in the cupboards and refrigerator keeps everything on display. At right, storage baskets for similar food groups offer convenience and aesthetic appeal.

LEFT Chicken wire placed between two pieces of glass is a nostalgic and stylish choice for the cupboards.

OPPOSITE The centerpiece of the kitchen is this rebuilt 1947 O'Keefe and Merritt Town & Country stove.

ABOVE Old-fashioned penny-candy containers hold raisins on the countertop.

BELOW LEFT The checkerboard ceramic tiles on the countertops and backsplash combine with a brick floor and rag rugs to form a framework for Kitty's collections.

INTERIOR DESIGNER: KITTY
    BARTHOLOMEW
COUNTERTOP: 2-BY-2-INCH BLACK AND
    WHITE TILES
DISHWASHER: "POTSCRUBBER" BY
    GENERAL ELECTRIC
FIXTURE: DORNBRACHT
FLOOR: BRICK WITH RANDOM ACCENTS
    OF PAINTED GREEN BRICKS
FREEZER: BEVERAGE AIR, COMMERCIAL
ICEMAKER: WESTINGHOUSE
REFRIGERATOR: CUSTOM COMMERCIAL BY
    VALIANT
SINK: STAINLESS STEEL
STOVE: 1947 O'KEEFE AND MERRITT
    TOWN & COUNTRY SIX-BURNER,
    THREE-OVEN STOVE FROM ANTIQUE
    STOVE HEAVEN
TROMPE L'OEIL ARTWORK: THE PAINTED
    LOOK

Personality in a Small Space

"I've found I can't eat in unattractive surroundings," says J. Allen Murphy. "I lose my appetite. So my kitchen is, I suppose, a fantasy."

Murphy moved from a large country house with an enormous kitchen and walk-in china closet to an apartment with a kitchen that measures a tiny 87 × 107 inches. He refused to be discouraged by the physical limitations of his new digs—and he rose to the challenge to make this very small room personable and functional at the same time.

First, Murphy came up with the plan of the kitchen mimicking a wet bar with a sliding pocket door. Taking a cue from his beloved "Napoleon Ivy" china (designed by Wedgwood, the china was originally used by Napoleon when he went into exile at St. Helena's), Murphy wallpapered the entire room in an overall ivy pattern that he had designed for Brunschwig & Fils.

To make the kitchen more workable Allen moved one wall back about three feet and moved the stove and sink into the new space. All appliances are standard size and there's still more than sufficient room for preparing food comfortably, without having to take unnecessary steps.

Multiple use is the key in this small space. The dining table, for instance, becomes a writing table or a place to telephone friends; a chair is drafted into service as a bar. Says the particular Mr. Murphy, "All in all, a very workable little kitchen."

Framed photographs documenting the owner's career as a journalist and designer personalize the impromptu bar at left; leopard velvet covers the Regency chair. With the efficiency of a yachtsman, the owner has succeeded in fitting much into a rather small space. The open shelving at right forms an eclectic backdrop for the small dining table.

ABOVE Murphy keeps a pot of ivy on the shelves with his "Napoleon Ivy" Wedgwood china.

BELOW The stacked washer/dryer is concealed behind a pair of doors hung with photographs.

ABOVE Everything in this kitchen is compact—from the stove, dishwasher, and sink to the tiny television.

BELOW The doors of a tiered Regency dining server hide detergents and other practical items underneath.

ABOVE A small oak box holds some favorite and well-worn recipes.

RIGHT A view from the hallway into the kitchen spotlights the Louis XV *semainier*, which is used to hold silver and linens.

INTERIOR DESIGNER: J. ALLEN MURPHY
ANTIQUES: THE ECLECTIC SHOP
COUNTERTOP: FORMICA
DISHWASHER: GENERAL ELECTRIC
FLOOR: MEXICAN TILE
LIGHTING: TRACK
REFRIGERATOR: HOT POINT
SINK: STAINLESS STEEL
STOVE: MAGIC CHEF
WALLS: BRUNSCHWIG & FILS "IVY"
  WALLPAPER
WASHER/DRYER: STACKABLE MAYTAG

Informality on All Levels

When asked how much time he spends in the comfortable and charming kitchen of his Santa Fe home, interior designer Thom Von Bulow says, "Lots! It seems, like most of my clients, I basically live in my kitchen and bedroom."

The Von Bulow house, designed for the previous owner by well-known architect Antoine Predock, is located at the top of a mountain and offers an extraordinary 360-degree view of the mountain ranges surrounding the Santa Fe basin. Predock made full use of these spectacular views by designing the solar house as a complete circle around an open courtyard. Von Bulow points out that the kitchen was built as the architectural center, ensuring its role as the focal point of life in the house.

"I'm the only one who cooks in this house—guests don't. But guests can be in the courtyard, the greenhouse, at the dining table, in the living room, or sitting in front of the fire, and because of the house's unique design, they are all part of the kitchen life."

The kitchen is multilevel, which not only breaks the space into different areas for prep work, cooking, cleaning, and dining, but also allows guests to perch on the brick steps during the informal entertaining that Thom most enjoys. And because nights in the desert are always cold, the fireplace burns year-round—plus it's large enough to hold a Tuscan grill for cooking. The little seating area in front of the fire is where Thom often breakfasts.

Santa Fe sun splashes into this mountaintop kitchen. A small butcher-block island at left holds knives, a circular condiment and spice shelf, and storage with easy access from three sides. Silver shakers at right illustrate the owner's penchant for collecting kitchenalia with a southwestern motif.

ABOVE Behind the cushioned seating area is shelving for cookbook and plate storage.

BELOW LEFT One comfortable level in this kitchen is the banquette across from the fireplace.

The spirit of the original kitchen is preserved, but to make it his own, Thom changed a few things. "The counters," he says, "were originally Formica, and that was really more architectural than I wanted. So to warm it up I put in some local tile." Thom is also a fan of American furniture and put it to great use in his own kitchen and dining area. He added the horse saddle, which he found in a local antique store, to the banquette. His walk-in pantry, attached to the kitchen, also has some Von Bulow touches with its extensive collection of salt and pepper shakers—each with a southwestern motif.

ABOVE Local tile with adobe grout is edged with a light wood—an unusual and informal touch.

RIGHT Another of the owner's design additions: a double-tiered condiment shelf handily placed beneath the hanging pot rack echoes the multiple levels of this room.

ARCHITECT: ANTOINE PREDOCK
INTERIOR DESIGNER: THOM VON BULOW
CABINETS: CUSTOM-BUILT PAINTED WOOD
COOKTOP: KITCHENAID
COUNTERTOP: CERAMIC TILE AND
    BUTCHER BLOCK
DISHWASHER: GENERAL ELECTRIC
FIXTURES: CHICAGO
FLOOR: BRICK
LIGHTING: RECESSED TRACK
OVEN: KITCHENAID
POT RACK: CUSTOM-DESIGNED BY THOM
    VON BULOW
PULLS: ARTISANOS
REFRIGERATOR/FREEZER: SUB-ZERO
SINK: ELKAY
WALLS: PLASTER

Professional

.... *Seasoned*
practitioners
of the kitchen
arts display
their wares

A Master's Choice

"I think my kitchen comes very close to being perfect," says Craig Claiborne—the internationally known food authority and author of sixteen cookbooks —of his East Hampton kitchen. After looking at his kitchen and learning how it works, we accept this revelation as fact, not bravado.

Craig did not come to his elevated position with ease. Born and raised in a Mississippi boarding house with numerous servants and marvelous cooks who introduced him to soul food, Craig didn't play sports, and so the kitchen became his playground. He was, in his own words, "horribly insecure with no ambition, but liked to write from the cradle on."

He started with pre-med, then went on to study journalism at the University of Missouri. World War II and the Navy took him to North Africa for the invasion. There he discovered that there was more to eating than Southern food. After the military, he attended the famed Professional School of the Hotel Keeper's Association in Lausanne, Switzerland. It was here that Craig "discovered" himself, and when he returned to New York, he worked briefly for *Gourmet* magazine and then became food editor for the *New York Times*.

Craig's kitchen in East Hampton incorporates knowledge accumulated over the years. Because of his culinary reputation, he is able to see the vast array of new products, equipment, and gadgets that floods the market each year, but he sticks to what works best for him. It took Craig—assisted by kitchen designer Vic-

Craig's marble-topped island is surrounded by the accoutrements of a food professional—a plethora of copper pots and a wall of stainless steel equipment—and the necessary tools of his trade—typewriter, telephone, and plenty of work space.

ABOVE White cookware stands out clearly against the dark blue undercounter storage. A stretch of pegboard keeps all sorts of kitchen gadgets within arm's reach.

ARCHITECT: WILLIAM ELLIS
DESIGNERS: VICTOR KASNER, CRAIG CLAIBORNE
CABINETS: STAINLESS-STEEL CUSTOM CABINETRY
COUNTERTOPS: MARBLE-TOPPED ISLAND; STAINLESS STEEL AND CORIAN
DISHWASHERS: HOBART AND HOBART'S ONE-MINUTE-CYCLE
FLOOR: CERAMIC TILE
LIGHTING: RECESSED LIGHTING, GLOBES BY PRIME LIGHT
OVENS: THERMADOR WALL OVEN; AMANA MICROWAVE OVEN; CUSTOM-BUILT INDIAN TANDOORI OVEN; CHINESE ROAST PORK OVEN
POT RACK: CUSTOM DESIGNED BY VICTOR KASNER
REFRIGERATORS: TRAULSEN; UNDERCOUNTER BY DELFIELD
SINK: PRICE-PFISTER
STOVE: GARLAND

tor Kasner—two years to get his kitchen organized and outfitted precisely as he needed and wanted it. "Efficiency, convenience, and ease in cooking when entertaining two to a hundred guests" is what inspired Craig to create this kitchen with its long galley layout. His main stove, complete with cooktop and oven, is a Garland; his wall oven is by Thermador, and his refrigerator is a Traulsen. He also had custom-made square stainless-steel garbage containers that can hold up to thirty gallons and are on casters for mobility. All his storage drawers automatically roll back and his countertops are stainless steel and Corian. The Corian was chosen for its eye appeal and the stainless for its professional look and for ease in cleaning. The pegboard, which he's had for years, is perfect for keeping small utensils organized and within quick and easy reach. The marble-topped island—used for cutting and storage, of course, but also the "desk" where Craig types his recipes, columns, and books—may be his favorite piece of furniture in this room.

Indeed, Craig's kitchen offers him what he most needs and wants for his work: organization and comfort. He spends an average of four hours a day here—much more when he is hard at work on a project. And of course this room, with its cedar walls and brick tile floor, serves as the staging area for his frequent parties. Among the most notable is his annual black-tie New Year's Day luncheon with "lots of caviar and champagne and leftovers from the night before, plus smoked salmon, sturgeon, herring, and bagels."

This connoisseur of the kitchen seems to have every necessary piece of kitchen equipment and much more, including a Chinese roast pork oven and a four-foot standing tandoori oven (which takes twenty-four hours just to heat up). But when pressed, what equipment could he not live without? "My food processors (he has no fewer than four Cuisinarts with different capacities), Chef's Choice knife sharpener, and GraLab electric timer which was originally designed for photography labs." And the best thing about his kitchen? Craig has no doubt about that: "My open and closed storage."

ABOVE Next to the Sub-Zero refrigerator is a handcrafted Indian tandoori oven with its own exhaust hood.

LEFT A separate library houses the writer's vast collection of cookbooks.

BELOW His Cuisinarts are among the equipment Craig finds essential.

Professional Minimalism

"Food and cooking are my passion. I've always felt it was my way to involve people in my home." The owner of this well-ordered Los Angeles kitchen got her initial inspiration for its renovation from her previous career as co-owner and administrator of the Ma Maison Cooking School. Together with Patrick Terrail (chef and founder of Ma Maison Restaurant), she had access to some of the best minds in the food world.

Among her responsibilities was seeking out new chefs. "One of the side benefits was that you could go to dinner in their restaurants one night, and be taught by them the following day. It was delicious!"

Now she will have the occasional chef in to her own kitchen to teach friends or for a fund-raising evening. She also works with FAITH (Family Assistance Involving The Homeless), which provides meals for the needy of Los Angeles. Her own kitchen works perfectly for these chefs. "What I learned from them and what strongly influenced me in designing my own kitchen is that simplicity, and not a lot of equipment or gimmicks, is what matters. A grill, a cooktop, ample counter space, and good knives are the key."

When she and her husband undertook the renovation, they collaborated with a contemporary architecture team who provided them with the shell. A counter seen in an old general store was the inspiration for their center island. Copied in maple butcher block and enameled in a bluish green, it has storage space in the back and pull-up seating on the other side.

Sunlight streaks across the open kitchen shelves. At right, the simple, yet professional lines of the U.S. Range and the hanging pots set the tone for this well-equipped kitchen. The double "C" curves of the stove can handle all sizes of pot.

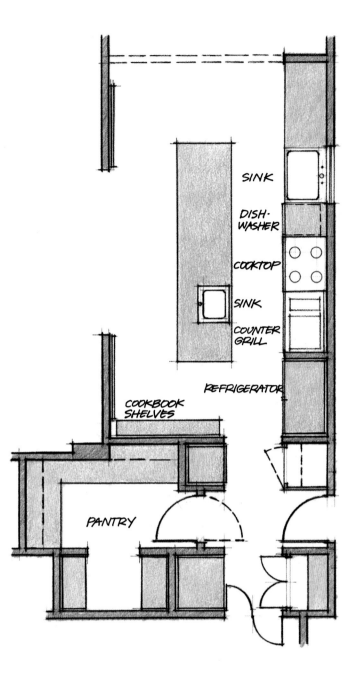

SINK

DISH-
WASHER

COOKTOP

SINK

COUNTER
GRILL

REFRIGERATOR

COOKBOOK
SHELVES

PANTRY

ABOVE An antique scale, salt shakers, and pepper mill sit on a slab of marble, which was added to one end of the counter and used when rolling pastry.

LEFT Glass barn doors, with duplicate bookshelves on either side, slide open to connect the kitchen to the rest of the house. Three bar stools straddle the counter with its painted tongue-in-groove paneling.

ARCHITECT: Koning-Eizenberg
BUILDER: Paster Construction
BACKSPLASH: granite
CABINETS: custom-designed
COOKTOP: U.S. Range
COUNTERTOP: wood, granite
DISHWASHER: Thermador
FIXTURES: Chicago
FLOOR: Oak
GRILL: Char-glo
LIGHTING: halogen
OVEN: Modern Maid
REFRIGERATOR/FREEZER: Sub-Zero
SINK: Elkay

RIGHT Open and closed shelves make great sense and supply plentiful storage space beneath this long center island.

BELOW Deep, adjustable wire shelving allows easy inventory of pantry supplies and supports a lot of weight.

Culinary Innovations

Restaurant consultant and cookbook author George Lang designed his New York City kitchen to replicate, spiritually, the kitchens of his native Hungary. In the early 1970s, Lang collaborated with architect Donald C. Mallow on the design of the kitchen in a space that was originally a studio, dining room, kitchen, and powder room. Among their innovations are the cut-in in the butcher block for discarding chopping waste and a vertical knife drawer—all are as up to date today as they were then.

The kitchen is designed in such a way that every member of the Lang family can play or work at the same time—a top priority in the master plan. There is a small office for George's wife, cookbook author Jenifer Lang, a play kitchen for son Simon and his friends, and a wine cellar where George can "play with cataloging my rare vintages." Jenifer is also managing director of George's restaurant, the Café des Artistes, and she uses the kitchen to test recipes for it.

Another of the important ingredients was versatility. For buffets, the credenza is designed with a built-in plate lowerater (a round opening with a spring mechanism that holds and warms sixteen plates) and built-in Salton heating units. And next to the range is a movable countertop, for easier access at buffets.

Reflecting the Langs' wide-ranging interests, the materials for the kitchen come from a great variety of places. The marble on top of the baking center is from

Beneath a slab marble countertop is a pull-out maple carving board. At right, pull-out plastic canisters for dry foodstuffs and a pull-out knife drawer that holds up to fifteen knives are just two of the innovative kitchen designs that Lang installed more than a dozen years ago.

Alabama, the blue tile facing the base of the counter came from Valleuris in France, the brass hood over the range from Hamburg, and the counter stools were made in Switzerland. Many of the elements—like the soda fountain, the Traulsen refrigerator and freezer, the Garland oven—are professional restaurant models.

And because George believes that "design determines behavior to a great degree—I'm glad that our son Simon's growing-up years will take place in our kitchen rather than in our living room."

George, a good friend of the late James Beard, remembers his famous friend's words of wisdom: "You can grow old and ugly but if you are a good cook, the world will still beat a path to your door." He adds: "Creating a great kitchen will serve as a well-paved road for the world at large."

OPPOSITE A comprehensive design plan by the owner was formulated to accommodate professional restaurant equipment—years before the surge in popularity of commercial equipment for residential use.

BELOW The temperature in this specially designed cabinet is thermostatically controlled to allow for ideal storage of wine.

ABOVE The detailing in the room—from the tiled backsplash to the beveled glass in the cabinet doors—helps create a comfortable look that is distinctly European.

ARCHITECT: DONALD C. MALLOW
INTERIOR DESIGNER: GEORGE LANG
CABINETS: CUSTOM-MADE WOOD WITH
    BEVELED GLASS
COOKTOP: CORNING
COUNTERTOP: MAPLE BUTCHER BLOCK
DISHWASHER: KITCHENAID
FLOOR: WHITE CERAMIC TILE
FREEZER: TRAULSEN
LIGHTING: CUSTOM DESIGNED
OVENS: GARLAND AND HOTPOINT
    CONVECTION OVEN
REFRIGERATOR: TRAULSEN

Maximum Production

Definitely not your standard fare, the Robyn Low and Bran Ferren kitchen was designed to look easygoing. At the same time, it functions at high gear. This futuristic kitchen, just minutes from the Atlantic Ocean, was added on to the original cottage by Bran, a well-known designer and an Academy Award nominee for Special Visual Effects for *Little Shop of Horrors* and *Star Trek V: The Final Frontier*.

As the kitchen plan evolved, Robyn—a caterer, food writer, and restaurant consultant—added the vital finishing touches: the huge portable pantry, the rolling prep table, and the restaurant-size pots and pans.

A great source of inspiration was the Restaurant Supply Show held each year in New York City. Another key ingredient was the book *Pierre Franey's Kitchen*, which guided them in stocking up their kitchen. Third was their own hard work and invention. In their search for the "best" wok stove, they discovered there is almost nothing written in English on the subject. After numerous forays into Manhattan's Chinatown, they found a manufacturer who built a stainless-steel wok to their specifications.

Before a plan was drawn or a nail was hammered, Bran thought through each need and chore. "I thought about tasks and the types of appliances and laid them out in a way that seemed most efficient. For instance, for a salad, I set up an area for washing and chopping vegetables. That then dictated that I would need a separate wooden-topped counter for chopping, refrig-

A low-glare industrial fixture at left illuminates a Panasonic Industrial 1600 microwave oven and a Ciamboli espresso maker on this extra-thick granite countertop. At right, an antique grocery scale and copper pots hang from the custom-designed hood. The copper tops are stored in a wooden plate rack.

erated drawers to store the vegetables underneath, and a sink right next to this prep work area. I ended up with three sinks in our kitchen because I also wanted a deep, separate sink near the dining room for dirty dishes, and a general-purpose sink." Bran also installed an industrial strength spray fixture for the deep sink and a Champion dishwasher—capable of washing a load of glassware and dishes in ninety-two seconds—in this corner of the kitchen. Robyn adds, "It's the ultimate setup for professional and home use, combining the best of both worlds."

Undoubtedly, the focal point in this 34-by-26-foot kitchen is the 8-by-6-foot Thirode stove from France, which is made up of two grills, a *bain marie* (hot water

bath), an oversized burner for large pots, a deep fat fryer, a griddle, two electric hot plates and two gas hot tops, both gas and electric cooktops, a char broiler, and its own water spigot. It sits on an orange base with custom-built drawers. Its companion piece, the enormous hood, was custom-crafted by Bran. With the multitude of grills, fryers, and broilers, there is the ongoing potential for producing a lot of smoke, grease, and heat. The unique hood design not only removes dirty air, it replaces it with the equivalent amount of clean air.

All of the cutting-edge appliances aside, Robyn insists that "even though it's a professional kitchen, I can still turn out a cozy dinner for two."

ABOVE The heart of this kitchen is the centrally positioned Thirode stove with its various work centers. Designed for accessibility on all four sides, it can be individualized according to each kitchen's requirements. The oak flooring, laid on an angle, was chosen for its aesthetic appeal and also for comfort underfoot.

ABOVE RIGHT Coated wire shelving offers convenient storage and adds to the industrial theme.

RIGHT An electric Italian sandwich maker by Milano is one of the many unusual appliances in this kitchen.

ABOVE Glassware is kept on the ultimate in lazy Susans. Wire shelving on wheels brings supplies to the chef.

LEFT A necessity in an oversized kitchen, a stainless-steel table on wheels has drawers and lots of storage underneath.

OPPOSITE Custom-built drawers underneath the Thirode stove can accommodate the size and weight of large pots and pans. Set on ball bearings, each drawer can handle 350 pounds.

BUILDER: ASSOCIATES & FERREN
CABINETS: LISTA INTERNATIONAL CORP.
COUNTERTOP: STAINLESS STEEL
DISHWASHER: CHAMPION
FIXTURES: CHICAGO AND KOHLER
FLOOR: OAK
LIGHTING: LARGE FIXTURES—
     METALARTE; HAND AND DOWN
     LIGHTS—CUSTOM BUILT, ITALIAN
     INDUSTRIAL; FLUORESCENT IN HOOD
     —GRAINGER
OVEN: WOLF CONVECTION
POT RACK: OWNER DESIGNED
REFRIGERATOR/FREEZER: TRAULSEN
SINKS: CUSTOM ORANGE AND STAINLESS
     STEEL
STOVE: THIRODE, CUSTOM STOVE
     HYBRID OF GAS AND ELECTRIC, AND
     PLUMBED WITH WATER
WINE COOLER: TRAULSEN

Old World

.... *Unfettered by modernity, these kitchens are quietly inviting*

European Influence

From the street, Jessica McClintock's home looks typical of the many grand old houses that grace this quaint and well-heeled San Francisco neighborhood. But inside the massive front door, any vestiges of resemblance to the other homes quickly fades. With the late afternoon sun streaming inside, playing patterns on the marble floors, antique fabrics, and lace throughout this home, one is immediately reminded of a French country house.

Jessica, who is originally from Maine, infuses her home and her kitchen with the special brand of romance and femininity that is the hallmark of the dresses that she's been designing for little girls and their mothers for over twenty years. Although her kitchen was created more than a dozen years ago with the help of interior designer Diane Burn, it is as timeless today as it was at its inception.

"I wanted an eighteenth-century French garden room with marble, natural wood, and hand-painted walls," Diane says. "I always have lots of flowers here —the little touches are very important to me in my life, my home, my clothing."

An overall, carefully coordinated design approach was the key. Jessica and Diane gutted the entire kitchen space. The walls were finished in a glazed plaster. The ceiling, painted by Charlie Campbell, is reminiscent of one in an old-fashioned French bakery but here it is covered with a sheet of Plexiglas. Countertops are a softly worn marble, and the hand-carved wood detailing on the cabinetry disguises such practi-

An oversized armoire, flowers, old baskets filled with fruit, a country table and benches—all combine to create the French garden mood that Jessica sought in her kitchen. The hood over the Wolf stove is hand-carved.

cal twentieth-century conveniences as the dishwasher, refrigerator, and freezer.

One of the largest pieces in the room, the pale pine armoire, holds china, silver, linens, and lace that Jessica has collected over the years. Another large piece, a hand-carved wooden work counter that was once a market counter in a French shop, houses the sink and fixtures; a great storage space hides behind its splendidly carved, pull-down door. The kitchen table—pine on a stone base—is also large. It's an ideal place for Jessica to work, whether it be cooking or designing dresses. The floor, a virtually indestructible château tile that improves with age, continues the European flavor of the room.

LEFT The walls are glazed plaster; the countertops, marble; the cabinetry, pine. A copper bar holds pots and pans. The baroque sconces are bedecked with dried fruits and flowers.

OPPOSITE A huge armoire provides stylish storage space for china and silver that the designer has collected in her travels.

BELOW The iron Art Nouveau chandelier hangs from the hand-painted ceiling, which is protected by washable Plexiglas.

ABOVE AND RIGHT An antique French market counter has been refitted with an Elkay sink and fixtures. The carved door pulls down to disclose great storage. Glazed and etched kitchen windows ensure privacy but can be angled for fresh air.

OPPOSITE AND BELOW Hand-carved panels disguise the Sub-Zero refrigerator and freezer. A television set fits compactly into the adjacent cabinet. Lace—Jessica's design trademark—is used as a curtain on the door leading to the dining room.

INTERIOR DESIGNER: DIANE BURN AND JESSICA MCCLINTOCK
ARCHITECT: TED EDEN
BUILDER: BOB GUNNELL
CABINETS: PINE, CUSTOM DESIGNED BY BOB GUNNELL
COUNTERTOP: MARBLE
DISHWASHER: KITCHENAID
FIXTURES: ELKAY

FLOOR: CHÂTEAU TILE
LIGHTING: SCONCES WITH BAROQUE ELEMENTS; IRON CHANDELIER
OVEN: WOLF
POT RACK: COPPER STANDING
PULLS: BALDWIN KNOBS, DISTRESSED
REFRIGERATOR/FREEZER: SUB-ZERO
SINK: ELKAY
WALLS: HAND-PAINTED GLAZED PLASTER

Country Comfort

When Randy and Bunny Williams began their kitchen renovation, their goal was to create an ambience that would be totally in keeping with the 200-year-old Federal-style house in historic Litchfield County, Connecticut, yet would still be comfortable to live in.

Bunny, an interior designer with her own firm, and Randy, an antiquarian book dealer, did some basic rearranging of windows and doors. By combining all the prep work equipment in an L-shaped area—which Bunny incorporates in many of her clients' homes—they also saved steps and separated themselves from the "living" part of the kitchen. "But the thing that makes the kitchen operate best," says Bunny, "is the big work table. This huge pine table was built in this room, and the previous owners couldn't remove it, so we inherited it."

Another basic and indispensable aspect of the kitchen is the deep, open shelving, which gives Bunny easy access to the pots and pans and bowls. "I really use those bowls, and I want to be able to quickly reach in and get what I'm looking for. I don't want to have to go to a cupboard and hunt around for something."

It was typical of the kitchens of that period to have a big fireplace with a bread oven next to it. The couple decided to keep theirs for its charm; it also balances the enormous island. They replaced the flooring with wide-planked pine, to keep the feel of the room, and covered the countertops with Formica, which Bunny likes because it is an "honest material." She edged it with stainless steel, which gives it an "old-fashioned feel, as if the kitchen has always been there."

While this room appears to have grown over time, it was completely revamped—only the huge pine island at right and the "Count Rumsford" fireplace remain in their original places. Majolica pottery fills the recessed niche next to the fireplace. A grained cabinet at left becomes a catchall for spices and condiments, brightening up an empty spot of wall.

ABOVE Because the huge work table couldn't be moved, the owners used it as the center of their kitchen, flanking it with L-shaped laminate countertops. Plates found on a trip to Portugal frame the double window; recessed high hats over the sink area and a brass English billiard-table lamp over the island provide plenty of task lighting.

OPPOSITE Soaps and brushes are kept handy in an old terra-cotta bowl by the sink.

RIGHT The drawers of the work island offer deep storage. An old American rag runner is used on the floor.

BELOW Oversized platters and trays are stored vertically in a cabinet between the stove and the refrigerator.

INTERIOR DESIGNER: Bunny Williams
CONTRACTOR: Warren and Macchi
CABINETS: custom built
COUNTERTOP: Formica with stainless-steel edge
DISHWASHER: General Electric
FIXTURES: Moen
FLOOR: wide-planked white pine
LIGHTING: down lights; brass billiard lamp from
    La Terrine
OVENS: Hardwick; General Electric wall oven
PULLS: Kraft
REFRIGERATOR/FREEZER: General Electric
SINK: Elkay

OVERLEAF The fireplace mantel is enlivened with personal mementos. A pair of miniature metal urns hold tiny topiaries. The clock is from the childhood kitchen of one of the owners. The framed decoupage pictures are old Victorian seed packets that Bunny acquired and assembled.

A Home for Found Objects

Asked when he first began renovation of the kitchen in his Hollywood Hills home—originally built in the 1920s by a British film actor as a hideaway for his mistress—Sandy Slepak remarks with his trademark deadpan face, "Work really began with my purchase of a sledgehammer."

Sandy, the well-known Hollywood costume designer (*Murphy Brown* is but one of his credits), calls his kitchen the axis of his home. It opens onto the foyer, dining room, living room, and garden. Because of this, he selected kitchen furniture that is decidedly "unkitcheny." "Imperfection interests me," says Sandy. "Antiques appeal to me because of their accumulated bumped and worn patina. The wooden surfaces show the signs of countless hands and feet." It is just that worn appeal that led him to his choice of furniture for this room.

A nineteenth-century English cricket table, for instance, has found new life as the kitchen table, and the two kitchen chairs are part of a set of six eighteenth-century English country chairs. His favorite piece—a nineteenth-century French painted wood-and-cane settee—is nestled into the corner of the kitchen with a view of the topiary garden. All three pieces were found at a friend's shop, G. R. Durenberger, in San Juan Capistrano.

And because the house is relatively small, each room needs to be as multifunctional as possible, with

An abundance of candlelight reinforces the low-key and eclectic charm of the Slepak kitchen. Barn siding, hanging lanterns, and old prints give definition to the room, while a mirrored refrigerator/freezer adds the illusion of space.

ARCHITECT: SPENCER DAVIES

INTERIOR DESIGNER: SANDY SLEPAK

BACKSPLASH: SQUARE MEXICAN TERRA-
COTTA TILE

CABINETS: CUSTOM-BUILT DOUGLAS FIR
PLANK

COOKTOP: THERMADOR

COUNTERTOP: HEXAGONAL MEXICAN
TERRA-COTTA TILE

DISHWASHER: KITCHENAID

FIXTURES: PRICE-PFISTER

FLOOR: HEXAGONAL MEXICAN TERRA-
COTTA TILE

LIGHTING: RECESSED DOWNLIGHTS

OVEN: THERMADOR

REFRIGERATOR/FREEZER: AMANA

SINK: ELKAY STAINLESS STEEL

WALLS: ROUGH-SAWN DOUGLAS FIR

LEFT A telling personal touch is Sandy's collection of antique keys—for doors and skates—and bottle openers.

BELOW Clever storage solutions are evident in this kitchen: a wooden plate rack on the countertop lets Sandy put away dishes while they're still wet.

ABOVE A pine arch hung with pots graciously opens the small kitchen into the dining area. The terra-cotta countertop with the Thermador cooktop strategically positioned at its center serves as a passway.

furniture to help fulfill its many roles. The settee in the kitchen is a cozy place for relaxing and reading; the cricket table, handy for board games and puzzles, is also a place to gather and visit with friends. Beside its everyday uses, the kitchen sink also serves as a location for Sandy's potting chores. The layout of the kitchen's tiny work area performs well. The center island table may take up a bit of space, but it saves steps at the same time. It also holds dozens of the old cooking utensils that Sandy collects. The wooden pine arch functions as a hanging pot rack, and the dining area's pantry doors —which are actually eighteenth-century French panels from a church—give the room a distinct Old World feeling.

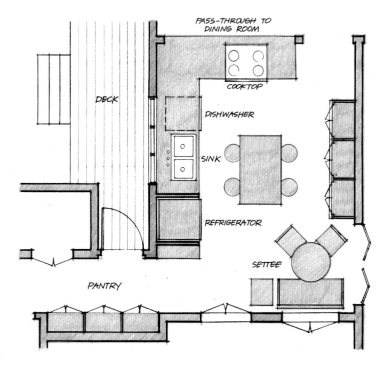

PASS-THROUGH TO DINING ROOM

DECK

COOKTOP

DISHWASHER

SINK

REFRIGERATOR

SETTEE

PANTRY

ABOVE Behind the double pair of eighteenth-century French panels—an effective backdrop for the dining area—are glassware, plates, and paraphernalia for entertaining. An antique three-paneled screen can be used to separate the room from the foyer.

RIGHT In the warmer summer months, with the French doors and windows open, the kitchen, eating area, and garden gently merge. In this view from the garden, with the kitchen work space on the right, the owner's love of old and worn objects is clearly visible.

BELOW The owner's favorite piece of furniture in the kitchen—the cane settee—nestles within the window. Covered with plump, mismatched pillows and a paisley throw, it allows guests to settle in luxuriously while Sandy cooks.

Chicly Unassuming

In the southern California town of San Juan Capistrano, antiques dealer and founder of the Decorative Arts Study Center G. R. "Gep" Durenberger lives stylishly in a one-story bungalow designed in 1928 by noted architect H. Roy Kelly. The house is "pure Gep" and it's become a favorite destination for many of Gep's good friends, including designers and decorators Sybil Connolly, John Saladino, Bill Blass, Mario Buatta, and other arbiters of taste.

Gep renovated the kitchen in 1977, but it maintains the Mediterranean feel that permeated the original design. His goal was to achieve a sense of comfortable informality and a lack of pretension or artifice. If the kitchen is, as he says, "long on charm but perhaps short on utility," that is perfectly fine, for it was never intended to be a "professional kitchen."

Gep was inspired by basic European kitchens, and the classic feel in his own arises from his selective use of antique tiles for the backsplash, old wooden countertops, a wooden floor painted over fifteen years ago and gently worn, a hammered copper sink, and such distinctive pieces as a Charles II armchair for a corner. Of special note is the old French apothecary cupboard, which was transformed into a cabinet, with drawers reworked into doors.

The kitchen was originally three little rooms. These were gutted, and vertical timber used to help define the space into two areas. The food prep area contains the stove, concealed refrigerator and pantry, an old

Durenberger's interest in European and American antiques is reflected throughout the room, especially in the cleanup and conversational area at left. The hand-painted cupboard is partially recessed into the wall and used to store crystal, spirits, and a miniature television set. At right, the beamed T separating the two work areas is highlighted.

ABOVE AND BELOW A converted French apothecary cupboard hangs over the butcher-block countertop work space. The drawers were reworked; they now function as door panels concealing shelves. The backsplash is of old Portuguese tiles.

American chopping block, and sink; the clean-up and conversational area has English chapel chairs, a French wine taster's table, a second larger sink, and a dishwasher.

Not only does the "triangle" at one end work exceedingly well—says Gep, who doesn't claim to be a cook—but the addition of the second entrance keeps the flow of guests moving smoothly, or in many cases, pitching in, in this jewel of a kitchen.

INTERIOR DESIGNER: GEP DURENBERGER

BACKSPLASH: ANTIQUE TILES

CABINETS: RECLAIMED

COUNTERTOP: OLD WOOD

DISHWASHER: GENERAL ELECTRIC "POTSCRUBBER 600"

FLOOR: PAINTED OAK

LIGHTING: ANTIQUE

REFRIGERATOR/FREEZER: SEARS

STOVE: GAFFER & SATLER

WALLS: PLASTER

ABOVE A corner work space comes to life with a beribboned tea cosy and fresh eggs laid that morning.

RIGHT The smallest details reinforce the antiquarian tone of this room.

BELOW A morning still life on a used butcher's chopping block. Gep cleverly attached a drop leaf of new butcher block for additional workspace.

ABOVE AND OPPOSITE A painted pine cupboard was converted into a dry sink. Lined with copper and fitted with an old French fixture, it is an important part of the food preparation area. Leaded glass windows were added during the renovation.

ABOVE Washed and worn cotton dish towels are stored in drawer.

LEFT The painted rough cedar not only covers the walls, but also conceals the refrigerator.

Seaside
Sentiment

Except for her grandmother's kitchen table, a new refrigerator, and a coat of paint, everything in this kitchen is exactly as the owners found it when they bought the nineteenth-century farmhouse in the mid-1970s. Located in a small village by the sea, it shows the effects of salt air and time.

In keeping with the owners' sentiments, the house is furnished to reflect a belief in the principle of "decorating with the found object." The couple, both of whom have demanding jobs in Manhattan, come here on weekends to relax.

"My husband and I were both small children in the forties, and we remember the houses, especially the kitchens, of that time. We found the kitchen in this state when we bought this house, and because of nostalgic as well as financial reasons, we decided to keep it old-fashioned. In fact, we love the room because it is so dated."

Over the years they have acquired simple kitchen furniture and old appliances at tag sales and flea markets. They are satisfied with the layout, but they do lament—as do owners of the most modern of kitchens —that they "could use a little more counter space." And in the pantry are the fruits of their September-weekend labors: jams, jellies, plum ketchup, tomato sauces, and corn relish.

At left, an American staple: a classic red laminate countertop edged in stainless steel. At right, the traditional farmhouse look is continued into the simple but not austere dining room.

ABOVE Simple kitchen tools. A sliver of space next to the stove works as improvised knife storage.

ABOVE A view from the kitchen toward the apple orchard. Hand-sewn gingham curtains frame the window.

BELOW The well-worn and rusted but still-working stove with a pair of homey kettles.

BELOW Old kitchen utensils in the pantry are not only collected, but also put to use.

ABOVE The owner's favorite piece from her grandmother's kitchen—a drop-leaf, enamel-topped worktable with storage beneath—holds a 1940s Nesco electric roaster.

Summer Colors

When Sally Quinn and Ben Bradlee first went through Grey Gardens—the historic, if somewhat crumbling, home they eventually bought in East Hampton—they saw an old-fashioned stove falling through the kitchen floor. Sally put her brand-new wood-burning stove in the same location, making it the focal point of their kitchen.

"The chimney was already there, which made it easier," explains Sally, a journalist and author. "I wanted to keep the look of what it once was—I wanted to re-create that feeling. Over the years, it had become four small rooms, and we brought it back to one large one. We also added wainscoting in the kitchen to keep that sense of age." Sally did most of the work herself with the assistance of an architect and contractor.

For entertaining small groups, Sally and her husband, Ben, long-time editor of the *Washington Post*, will set the food buffet-style on the counter near the bar sink. When caterers take over the kitchen for large parties, they move the sofas out and a breakfast table in to then function as an impromptu work area.

Because it is used by the family as a summer kitchen—with friends, children, dogs, bathing suits, sand, and all that they entail—Sally knew the kitchen had to be large. "I suppose if I were a serious cook, I would have wanted an efficient U-shaped kitchen with an island in the middle. But it wouldn't have looked nearly as good, and I didn't want to sacrifice aesthetics.

"I made the trade-off of a cook's professional kitchen for my living room kitchen with its three blue sofas and much-used stove. And, during the final nights of August with the first chill of fall in the air, we always have a fire going in the kitchen."

A black wood-burning stove anchors this country kitchen designed for both comfort and cooking.

ABOVE Open shelves and an understated window treatment contribute to the airy, relaxed feeling of this room.

OPPOSITE The owners deliberately sought to recapture the original feeling in the kitchen with tongue-in-groove paneling for the walls and plain white ceramic tile for the countertop. Much of the original cabinetry was recycled.

ABOVE A pitcher for lemonade, a basket for muffins—these are details that speak of home.

BELOW The bar sink also doubles as a work sink for the owners' extensive gardens. The glass panels in the cupboard doors are backed with simple shirred curtains.

ARCHITECT: Eugene Futterman
CONTRACTOR: Robert Langman
BACKSPLASH: plaster
CABINETS: custom-made
COOKTOP: Chambers
COUNTERTOP: ceramic tiles
DISHWASHER: KitchenAid
FLOOR: oak
LIGHTING: antique brass light fixtures
OVEN: Caloric
REFRIGERATOR/FREEZER: KitchenAid
SINK: Just
WALLS: Benjamin Moore "Linen White"

Resources & Inspiration

Today's Kitchen

The biggest revolution in kitchen design has been blending this room with the rest of the house. What was once considered a strictly utilitarian space—hidden behind closed doors and disconnected from other rooms—has become a full-fledged member of the home's design scheme.

This is markedly different from the view espoused by one of the earliest practitioners of what we now call "home economics." Catherine Beecher, who in 1841 wrote *A Treatise on Domestic Economy for the Use of Young Ladies at Home and at School*, was concerned not a whit with the style and fashion of the kitchen; instead she discussed how that room functioned most efficiently and economically in the day-to-day life of the home. It is different, too, from the concept of the kitchen as fantasized at the 1939 New York World's Fair. That kitchen—a highly automated, almost depersonalized laboratory—has never materialized.

What has evolved is the notion of the kitchen as the heart of the home. It is a room that reflects the lives, interests, and tastes of its owner or owners, while certainly utilizing the technological advances in cooking and cleaning vi-

sualized at the 1939 World's Fair. It is very much a room of comfort, warmth, and personality. Today we are decorating our kitchens in a way that up until now was reserved for the other rooms in the house: pairing a professional-style appliance, like a Garland stove, with a French armoire or a stripped Irish dresser filled with white-on-white crockery. You're now as likely to see elaborately framed art and comfortable upholstery as not. Or you might see poster-sized pictures of every member of the family. Clutter is not only tolerated in today's kitchen, it is often a welcome, joyful sign that somebody lives there.

Quite simply, times have changed, and the way we live at home, and in our kitchens, has changed with them. Many of us now spend 60 to 70 percent of our waking hours at home in the kitchen, so naturally the design of this room has been influenced by our changing lifestyles and habits. We tend to congregate as a family in this room—entertaining friends, sipping a predinner glass of wine, overseeing our children while they do homework. And yes, we do prepare our meals here. In this transition, we've been immeasurably aided and abetted by the plethora

BELOW Bookshelves and upholstered chairs create a comfortable corner, perfect for visiting friends.

of state-of-the-art developments in kitchen design and appliances over the past fifty years. But we haven't allowed new technology to overwhelm us.

We take advantage of these electronic marvels, but our sense of aesthetics still rules—within reason. Instead of having row upon row of slick, anonymous cabinets, which were so prevalent in the eighties, to surround our appliances, we have relaxed our design approach. For instance, we married high-performance appliances with an overstuffed armchair for recipe reading, a vintage linoleum floor, or, perhaps, a hand-carved wooden panel for the front of a Sub-Zero refrigerator/freezer.

Hand in hand with this revolutionary change in the role of the kitchen in our lives is the introduction of the kitchen as a central player in the design aesthetic of the house. Today, the flow of the house can emanate from the kitchen as much as from the entrance hall. This, as much as anything, has dictated a change in the way we decorate our kitchens. In older homes and apartments, we break down walls, and in newer residences, we open up the space to incorporate the kitchen into the center of the family's lifestyle. A design style or color scheme introduced in the living room or foyer is often carried through to the kitchen. A cherished collection or assemblage of memorabilia once at home only in a library or study

might very well today show up in the kitchen.

Design elements formerly found in other rooms in our homes have, in recent years, become familiar ingredients in kitchen design. Cultured marble, hand-painted ceramic tiles, exotic woods and finishes, hand-blown glass mullions, and antique decorative elements all exemplify this trend. As veteran kitchen designer Florence Perchuk explained recently, "Kitchens reflect what is going on in home furnishings and are designed today with all sorts of furniture pickling, enameling, marbling, and finishes painted on cabinets. Kitchen cabinets have actually become far more a piece of furniture."

In the kitchens I've found for this book, I've seen numerous examples of this very approach. The Bradlee/Quinn kitchen on Long Island, for instance, literally creates a second living room area with its comfortable sky-blue sofas and overstuffed pillows, all anchored by a woodburning stove; it continues the relaxed, informal summerhouse feel that permeates the rest of their home. Then there are southern Californian kitchens, which in many cases relate to the lush surroundings that are so integral to the design of homes in this area, and the Freymiller house in Rancho Santa Fe is no exception. This is a kitchen that was renovated with the specific idea of bringing the outdoors into the

ABOVE With its big, welcoming sofas and its wood stove, the Bradlee/Quinn kitchen is almost a living room.

BELOW The *equipal* chairs and the brightly colored throw on the pedestal table continue the southwestern theme of the Berry kitchen.

ABOVE An old American chopping block is given the place of honor in Gep Durenberger's kitchen.

BELOW The French painted settee in Sandy Slepak's kitchen is "decidedly unkitcheny."

heart of the room, and with its double set of French doors flung open much of the year, it strongly succeeds. And the outdoor theme set in the kitchen continues: harvests of herbs from the Freymillers' gardens are hung to dry not only in the kitchen, but in many rooms throughout the house. And with the kitchen seen on page 26, guests can wander from the stylish living room into the kitchen and bar area, mix a drink or two, with no diminution in the elegance and panache that permeates all the rooms of this Manhattan penthouse.

To such inveterate collectors of antiques like Gep Durenberger or Sandy Slepak, kitchens are as important as living rooms, studies, or dining rooms as places to display fine collections of European and American pieces. For instance, Sandy made a point of selecting kitchen furniture that was, as he put it, "decidedly unkitcheny." His kitchen table is a nineteenth-century English cricket table, and a French painted wood-and-cane settee is part of its seating. Gep took three little rooms and turned them into two connected kitchen areas, filling them with an old American chopping block, English chapel chairs, and a French apothecary cupboard. Turn the corner into his dining room and you'll see the same design aesthetic here and in the rooms beyond.

Arnelle Kase's capricious collections show up in every room of her home, and just one look at her kitchen (page 158) tells you that this is a home filled with warmth, intelligence, and whimsy. And it doesn't stop at the kitchen door. In Karin Blake's kitchen in Martha's Vineyard, basic appliances combine with pure white walls to showcase her simple yet gloriously colorful early American pieces. These strong shapes can be found in every room of her home. The strict design aesthetic that Andrée Putman has brought to a New York apartment is definitely found in its kitchen.

Details are the special ingredient that give kitchens personality, and the one important element that can take your kitchen from ordinary to a very special gathering spot in your home. This is a place to let yourself and members of your family shine. Think about your specific interests, and figure out how to incorporate them into this room. Whether your way is to scour flea markets and antique shows, or to incorporate old family mementos and treasures, or to hang your children's artwork on the refrigerator or in Lucite boxes on one wall, you can make your kitchen unique and relate it to the look and feeling of your home's other rooms.

The special touches that I discovered on my trips to kitchens throughout America run the gamut. Small wicker baskets used to store silver and other kitchen paraphernalia. An old handsome

terra-cotta bowl holding soap bars and steel wool. Antique silver napkin rings inscribed with various names are the artifacts that the entire Dunst family searches out in their travels to antique shops and markets throughout the world. Kitty Bartholomew's children know when they reach for the peanut butter in the fridge, they can also pull out the jam, since both jars are housed with the bread in the same wicker basket. The decorative elements in the Berry kitchen are the fruits of that day's harvest—pumpkins one day, chilies the next. And perhaps Craig Claiborne's kitchen "look" is the most simple and practical of all— a pegboard, brightly decorated and hung with all those odd-shaped kitchen tools that most of us never know where to store.

So what does this all mean for you? Well, whether it's a total gut job or a simple, cosmetic renovation, keep in mind all of the above. Don't be afraid to try something a little different for this room. Try to think about furnishing this room as you would the other rooms in your home. Borrow a piece of furniture from the living room; adding a comfortable armchair to a kitchen corner for cookbook reading might be just the homey touch you want. Reinforce it with a basket filled with magazines and paperbacks to pick up and dip into. You might actually find yourself sitting down and really enjoying this reading nook in your kitchen.

All of this accessorizing can, of course, be left to the end of your kitchen job, but a little foresight on your part can actually give you enough space to add some of these soft touches. In the following sections, you'll begin to get a sense of how to work with your contractor or kitchen planner or builder, but forewarned is forearmed. Bring to the table your dreams, wants, and needs. Planning to remodel will fill your mind with things you already knew and some things you might not have thought of. Familiarize yourself also with the choices in appliances, cabinetry, sinks, and faucets in the Visual Resources section and see how you can mix and match these elements to achieve your own personal look. You'll find that the Directory is an excellent guide to some of the top names in this business, as well as to some special finds that you should know about for this job— be it big or small. And, of course, try to remember that it's really *only* a kitchen.

ABOVE AND BELOW Collections can set the tone for a kitchen. Tropical bird pitchers are without a doubt whimsical; silver napkin rings are more elegant.

Planning to Remodel

It's one thing to be dissatisfied with your current kitchen, still another to know exactly what you want it to become. Planning is essential, for once the elements are in one place—appliances, cabinets, countertops, sinks—it's arduous to make significant changes. Mistakes mean money, and you don't want to endure a costly renovation only to realize what has been done is not quite what you need.

To reduce the margin for error or miscalculation, consider hiring a professional to give you sound guidance. He or she can't remodel your kitchen properly without knowing what you want, but a pro can certainly tell you if what you want is realistic. Consider every possibility. The more carefully you plan, the better—more useful, more economical, more responsive to your needs—your new kitchen will be.

Here are the steps to follow throughout the planning stage, before the first hammer blow is struck:

■ Measure your kitchen and everything in it. With graph paper and a straight edge, make a detailed floor plan to scale. Show the overall size and shape of the space, the location of each door and which way it swings, the size and placement of windows and skylights (if any), the location of appliances, plumbing fixtures, and cabinets. Once the plan is completed, you can mentally begin to shuffle the elements around and formulate how your kitchen could be improved.

■ Set your plan aside and do a detailed assessment of the kitchen—on lined paper with a line drawn down the center. On the left, note what's right about your kitchen—its location, perhaps, its proximity

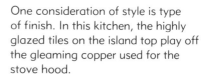

One consideration of style is type of finish. In this kitchen, the highly glazed tiles on the island top play off the gleaming copper used for the stove hood.

to the dining room or family room, whatever. On the right, list each flaw, each item that cries out to you for improvement.

- Analyze each flaw and start thinking about how you might correct it. Is the kitchen's size a problem? Its layout? Do you have sufficient light? Is storage adequate? Take time to measure your storage needs so you have a clear idea of how much additional cabinetry or storage space you need.

- Decide how, ideally, your new kitchen will be used. Will it be a gathering place for the family, the heart of your home when you entertain friends? If you don't have one now, do you want a place for family breakfasts or snacking? Do you want space for two cooks to work at one time? Do you need more food preparation surfaces—deeper counters, or perhaps an island work space? Make a "want list" to take to whatever professionals you consider hiring. Do you need more ovens? A cooktop instead of a stove? A microwave? Appliance garages for your toaster, blender, processor, coffeemaker? Two dishwashers instead of one? Note all these needs on your list.

- Style goes hand in hand with kitchen design. Know what you prefer in terms of cabinet design—do you want contemporary or traditional, natural wood or painted surfaces? If painted, what color? And what color would you like to see on walls and trim, or would you

YOU AND YOUR CONTRACTOR

The most important element in your relationship with your contractor is *trust*. By the time the project is completed, your contractor will probably know more about your life than your in-laws do. Since creating a successful project does not offer the luxury of time for second-guessing every decision or question, you must trust that the contractor has your best interests in mind.

The easy part of this is that most successful contractors are trustworthy. Since contractors do business, in most cases, within a fixed community, an untrustworthy contractor's reputation will soon become apparent and his business will die.

There are, of course, many people who still think they have found a deal and discovered this wonderful "Old World craftsman" who is going to build them the Taj Mahal and charge them for a doghouse. These are the same people who play three-card monte on the sidewalks of big cities.

How do you find a trustworthy contractor? Word of mouth is one tried-and-true way, but any way is all right as long as you remember the most important step in the selection process: get references and check them. Any contractor who won't give references either is hiding something or is not that interested in your job. Either way, you don't want him.

From the very beginning, it is important to spend time with your contractor, even if it is only discussing the weather. Go and see some of his jobs—preferably with him. Listen to him describe the job. Then call back the references and requestion them.

Now that you have found a trustworthy contractor, how do you conduct your relationship? With *communication, communication,* and *communication.*

Sign a contract, even if it is only a letter of agreement. This should spell out very carefully the scope of the work. It is most easily done if there are drawings and specifications from an architect, but even if the project is small, this can be done.

The agreement should also include timing and method

of payment. Progress payments create logical points for the owner and the contractor to resolve disputes before they become major. This precludes ever having to go to court except as a last resort. This discipline at the beginning of a job will pay many dividends later.

Specifications are very important. There are very good quality doorknobs available at approximately fifteen dollars each, and there are high-quality doorknobs at sixty dollars each. If this is not specified at the time of bidding and there are ten doors, you certainly can't blame the contractor for installing the fifteen-dollar knobs.

The scope of work and the specifications are most important at the time of bidding, also. Unscrupulous contractors love to see plans on the "back of an envelope." These bidders look very inexpensive until you find out what they are not including.

As the project progresses, your contractor has the responsibility of giving you all the options—not just the easiest or most cost effective for him. You can elicit these options by gently prodding him with questions such as, "What else can we do?" or "What would you do?" Help the contractor by making decisions as soon as you can. He, however, should leave you enough time for anything major so you can discuss this with your spouse, your architect, and whomever.

Make progress payments in a timely fashion. Your contractor has weekly wages and subcontractors who are after him for money quickly. Even vendors do not have the luxury of giving extended terms to the contractors. Eliminating the hassle of collecting money gives the contractor and his subs more time to devote to your job.

Make any change orders in writing. In the real world, this doesn't always happen, but communication is important. You should elicit the cost from the contractor as soon as possible, and he should include this change of cost in his next requisition for a progress payment. Here is an opportunity to resolve a dispute before it festers.

Take the time at the end of the job to prepare a realistic and complete "punch list." This makes it easier for the contractor. He realizes what he has to do, and he can

rather have wallpaper? Your color preferences may influence your choice of flooring, for you will have to decide whether to order wood, tile, or vinyl and, at the same time, pick what material in which color you'll want for countertops and backsplashes. You needn't make finite choices at this stage, but you should be able to identify what you like and what you'd like your new kitchen to have.

■ Work out a budget. Based on your own financial resources or your ability to obtain a second mortgage or home equity loan, decide what you will be able to spend to improve the kitchen. Keep in mind how much, realistically, you should spend—a plausible maximum. If recovering the cost of your new kitchen would make your house the most expensive one on your block, you might want to scale down your aspirations and trim your budget. While a new kitchen will make your house more marketable, whenever you wish to sell it, you cannot assume that you'll recoup every dollar you spend to improve it. If you plan to remain in your house at least three years after the renovation is finished, because of accelerated appreciation you can count on recovering about 85 percent of the cost. If you decide to sell in less than a year, however, you may lose your investment.

■ A contractor is the person you'll rely on to execute your remodeling plan, but before he enters the picture you may want to consult an architect, architectural designer, kitchen planner, or interior designer. Talk to at least three candidates before making a decision. With your master plan and want list in hand, you'll enable any professional you consult to suggest how your vision might be realized and how much it might cost.

■ Review the submission from each professional—the design ideas as well as the budget. These proposals plus your own assessment of how well you and that person relate will help you decide whom to hire. Even after you make a choice, you may ask to have the plan revised more than once. Take your time, and don't be dissuaded. It's far better to make changes on paper than to change direction after construction has begun.

■ Before you give a professional the go-ahead, make sure you agree on a sensible work schedule. Make sure, too, that while work is under way, you still have the ability to cook and refrigerate food, and that there is room outside your kitchen for storing utensils, supplies, and staples. More than you may realize, and regardless of its current condition, your kitchen really is the heart of your home. During the weeks when it's torn apart, you will definitely feel a sense of loss. The hope is that, when the last screw is turned and the touchup paint is finally dry, your new kitchen will be exactly what you have always wanted.

attack this list point by point and know at the completion that he will have a happy customer—and his money.

And, of course, as in all of life, respect for the workers is very important. If you project the feeling that their work is not very important, they will feel exactly that way themselves. This means you should extend compliments, be on time for appointments, and offer a "nice word" to the person who answers the worker's phone—be it secretary or spouse—should you have to call them for any reason. Last but not least, a smile and an offer of refreshment go a long way. All contractors have heard this from their subcontractors or employees: "I did something extra for the Smiths because they are very nice people."

A good contractor and every one of his workers or subcontractors are interested in having a happy customer and in doing a good job. They like to sleep well at night, are proud of their craftsmanship, and realize that doing the job right the first time is the most productive way.

Peter J. Whelan, contractor
Whelan Company, Rye, New York

YOU AND YOUR KITCHEN PLANNER

1. When meeting with a planner, bring a basic floor plan of what exists, a list of what you would like to change, and pictures of ideas that you might like to incorporate in your new kitchen.
2. Your kitchen planner will then come to view your present kitchen and see if your ideas are possible.
3. Your kitchen planner will coordinate your thoughts and ideas with the setting.
4. Plans will be drawn up.
5. Budget and prices will be given.
6. Your kitchen planner will then oversee the construction of your kitchen.

David Londin, kitchen planner
Kitchen Concepts, Harrison, New York

What the Pros Have to Offer

An architect or architectural designer will tell you which walls can be moved without compromising your structure. If additional supports are needed, this pro will design and position them. Based on careful on-site evaluations, he or she will be able to remedy any other structural defects that exist. Once you and your architect, or architectural designer, have agreed on what will be done to the kitchen —based on what truly *can* be done to it—he or she will draft a master plan. This plan will show every step your renovation will take—relocating appliances and plumbing fixtures according to your cooking needs, for example—and also will specify the materials and products to be ordered. You definitely need an architect if you plan major alterations or any addition that involves the exterior of your home. Plans for such work must be approved by the building department or planning commission in your community. To receive approval and, ultimately, that all-important certificate of occupancy, certified working drawings containing the architect's seal must be submitted, often accompanied by an engineer's report. An architect's drawings must be so clear and so explicit that the contractor you hire has no choice but to comply with them.

Some interior designers know and understand kitchens through years of experience, but kitchen planners are specialists. Kitchens should be the stock in trade of whomever you eventually deal with, someone able to diagnose problems and offer solutions that might not occur to anyone else, yourself or your contractor. A kitchen specialist should be able to

What the Initials Mean

As you consider the services of the various professionals, you'll come across some initials. Here's what they mean.

AIA: American Institute of Architects
This is the national professional organization for architects, with chapters across the country. Write the national office at 1735 New York Avenue NW, Washington, DC 20006 for more information.

CKD: Certified Kitchen Designer
The certification comes from the National Kitchen & Bath Association, which will provide a list of CKDs in your area. Write them at 687 Willow Grove Street, Hackettstown, NJ 10780.

CGR: Certified Graduate Remodeler
The Remodelers' Council of the National Association of Home Builders will provide a list of CGR contractors in your area. Write them at 15th and M Street NW, Washington. DC 20005.

CR: Certified Remodeler
Send a self-addressed stamped envelope to the National Association of the Remodeling Industry, 1901 N. Moore Street, Arlington, VA 22209, for a list of CR contractors near you.

suggest how your current space can be put to better use, pointing out which products would satisfy your cooking needs and improve efficiency. Finally, a specialist can help you decide where and how to spend money for the most positive, fulfilling results.

A contractor is comparable to the conductor of an orchestra, a person of many skills and talents who coordinates the skills and talents of many others. A contractor is, at various times, a master builder, troubleshooter, shrewd shopper, and manager, someone organized well enough to get the most work done in the least amount of time. It is his responsibility to engage the demolition crew that will knock down walls and to find and hire the plumber, electrician, carpenter, and painter who will be involved in new construction. The contractor orders materials, sees to the comings and goings of subcontractors, applies for your building permit, deals with the local bureaucracy, schedules inspector visits as needed so work in progress can be approved, and directs his building crew. Most important, a contractor solves the many problems that invariably arise on a job. He appears at the site daily to make decisions and reevaluations, and maintains the building schedule he has promised so the work is completed on time. Also, he should make himself available to you whenever you have questions or concerns.

NUTS AND BOLTS

There are no easy step-by-step installation instructions for kitchen renovation. The use of different materials to perform the same task makes the preparation and installation vary in accordance with the demands of your specific situation. For example, a wood-frame house with plaster on wood lath will differ from work in a wood-frame house with sheet rock. *The best plan for installation is to have the most thorough preparation.*

- Start by stripping the room: take out the previous cabinets, remove the floor covering back to the original subflooring, and rip off the plaster or sheet rock to reveal rough framing.
- Correct any structural problems: set new windows, remove walls, and construct new wall.
- Have *licensed* plumbers and electricians form rough-in work. Protect yourself. *Have the work inspected.*
- Insulate all exposed wall, floors, and ceilings.
- Replace the subflooring.
- Install either plaster walls or sheet rock and at least first coat of taping.
- Position and set new cabinets by leveling each individual unit and screwing it to the walls and the adjacent cabinets. Start from the inside corners and work out.
- Set your countertops and backsplash.
- Complete the second and third coat of taping.
- Install the finished floor.
- Set finished moldings on doors, windows, and baseboards.
- Install finished light fixtures and appliances, and test them.
- Paint and/or wallpaper.

David Londin, kitchen planner
Kitchen Concepts, Harrison, New York

Visual
Resources

There are countless options for you to consider when you set about redoing your kitchen. In the pages that follow, I've tried to give you enough information to spur your imagination. You might never have considered using antique cabinets to showcase your glassware, for example, or fitting drawers for wine storage. You'll be able to see at a glance any number of options for sinks and fixtures, to compare cooktops with stoves, and to consider a variety of flooring materials. Check the Directory for addresses of manufacturers of specific products that interest you, and write for the location of outlets near you.

Cabinetry: Freestanding

1. A white pine triple cabinet.
2. White enamel-finish cabinets with a glass insert.
3. A small unfitted piece recycled for use as a spice cabinet.
4. A large American freestanding cupboard.
5. A small unfitted pine cupboard.
6. An industrial metal and glass cabinet.
7. An oversized early American cupboard with four doors.
8. A small unfitted cabinet from Smallbone, Inc.
9. An old pine breakfront.
10. An antique dental supply cabinet recycled for kitchen use.

1.

4.

2.

3.

7.

5.

6.

10.

8.

9.

Cabinetry

1. "Euro 6." European-style cabinetry from KraftMaid Cabinetry, Inc.
2. "Brittany" cabinetry from Timberlake Cabinet Co.
3. Painted cabinets from Smallbone, Inc.
4. Stock cabinets from Ikea.
5. "Country Traditions" cabinetry from Quaker Maid.
6. Cabinets and island from Siematic Kitchens.
7. Furniture grade stainless-steel cabinetry from St. Charles.
8. Custom European-style cabinetry from Wood-Mode.
9. "English Manor" cabinetry from Rutt Custom Kitchens.
10. Compact kitchen from Sears, Roebuck and Company.
11. Stock cabinets from Ikea.
12. Stock cabinets from Ikea.

1.

2.

3.

4.

5.

6.

7.

8.

9.

10.

11.

12.

Cabinetry: Shelving

1. Above the stock wood-and-steel pot-hook system are heavyweight glass shelves.
2. An old painted kitchen dresser is used to store a collection of wooden plates and glasses.
3. A built-in hutch holds serving pieces and accessories.
4. A pantry has been fitted with an industrial wire shelf unit.
5. Very narrow shelves have been added to a structural column.
6. A brass pot rack with stainless-steel hooks.
7. A strip of lathe fitted with C-hooks.
8. Bi-fold pantry storage.
9. Classic open shelving, cup hooks and all.

1.

2.

3.

4.

5.

6.

7.

8.

9.

Cabinetry:
Drawers

1. A trio of deep drawers.
2. "Bread-box" drawer from Rev-A-Shelf.
3. A lazy Susan corner.
4. A corner cabinet fitted with a double-decker lazy Susan.
5. Narrow drawers fitted to store wine (see page 196).
6. Recycling drawers from Rutt.
7. Half-circle rubber-coated wire pullouts.
8. Narrow pull-out pantry.
9. Pull-out bread board.
10. Tip-out sink-front storage from the Rev-A-Shelf line.
11. A tip-out trash cabinet.
12. Universal spice-tray drawers from Rev-A-Shelf.
13. Pull-out towel bar from Rev-A-Shelf.
14. Custom undercounter storage.
15. ADS Aluminum drawer system from MEPLA, Inc.

1.

2.

3.

4.

5.

6.

7.

9.

10.

8.

12.

11.

13.

14.

15.

Cabinet and Drawer Pulls

1. Custom iron pull.
2. A simple brass pull.
3. A new iron key made to look old.
4. Scrolled brass pulls.
5. A variety of pulls and finishes from Green Street Details.
6. Flat enameled metal pulls.
7. Cabinet and pulls from Boffi.
8. Wooden half-moon drawer pulls from Smallbone, Inc.
9. Custom animal pulls from Chris Collicot.
10. A flea market find.
11. A brass ring pull.
12. New brass pulls from Baldwin.
13. New brass pulls from Kraft.
14. Painted reproduction Shaker pulls.
15. The Strothmann line of decorative handles from Hettich America.
16. Custom knobs from Smallbone, Inc.
17. Vintage ceramic pulls.

1.

2.

3.

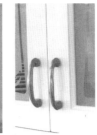

4.

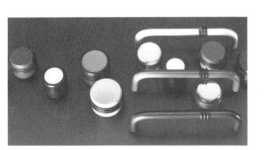

5.

6.

7.

8.

9.

10.

11.

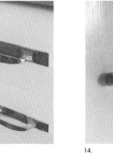

12.

13.

14.

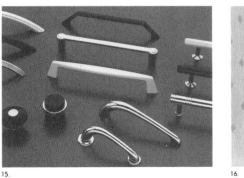

15.

16.

17.

Countertops

1. Avonite "Crystelle."
2. Five different edge finishes from Avonite.
3. "Gemstone" and "Marble" finishes from Avonite.
4. Granite patterns in Surell from Formica Corp.
5. Metal laminates from Formica's International Collection.
6, 7, and 8. Three integrated sink worktops combine Corian sinks with countertops—all from DuPont.
9 and 10. Two applications of Fountainhead by Nevamar.
11. "Black crystal" veneer from Gramitech.
12. Three different edge finishes with Nevamar Fountainhead.
13. "Plexability" from Avonite.

1.

2.

3.

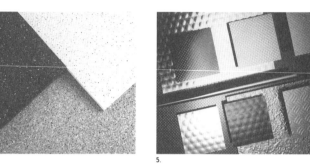

4.   5.

6.   7.   8.

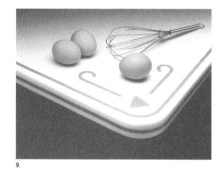   

9.   10.

11.   12.   13.

Countertops

1. A variety of decorative tiles from the Italian Tile Council.
2. Busby-Gilbert white tile trimmed with barn wood (see page 64).
3. "Terrestrial" wall and countertop tiles with accents from Wenczel Tile Company.
4. Black and white ceramic tiles in a checkerboard pattern (see page 174).
5. A highly glazed ceramic tile.
6. A maple butcher-block counter with painted wood edging.
7. Bleached teak countertop.
8. Old Dutch hand-painted tile from Amsterdam Corporation.
9. Wooden corner molding from Wilsonart.
10. Granite countertop.
11. Glazed Mexican tile.
12. "Deco-Block" interlocking glass bricks from Outwater.
13. Stainless-steel counter and backsplash.

1.

2.

3.

4.

5.

6.

7.

8.

9.

10.

11.

12.

13.

Sinks

1. A stainless-steel sink with enameled wire basket and companion cutting board from Abbaka.
2. Hand-hammered copper basin.
3. A small porcelain model from Kohler.
4. A small prep sink set into an island.
5. An Elkay sink set in white Florida tile.
6. A small sink from Franke.
7 and 8. Two unusually shaped kitchen basins from Kohler.
9. A Franke sink set into a granite island.
10. The "Entertainer," with two trays and cutting board, from Kohler.
11. Kohler's "Porto Fino" sink.
12. A bar sink with custom mirror finish from Abbaka.
13. Rectangular bar sink from Abbaka.
14. Circular brass bar sink from The Broadway Collection.
15. Square brass bar sink with blade handles from Barclay Products.

1.

2.

3.

4.

5.

6.

7.

8.

9.

10.

11.

12.

13.

14.

15.

Sinks

1. A Blanco "Classic" stainless-steel sink.
2. A "Progresso" stainless-steel sink from Franke.
3. "New Madrigal" stainless-steel sink from Kohler.
4. Extra-deep sink from Kohler.
5. Stainless-steel sink from Kindred Industries.
6. Custom stainless-steel sink.
7. A quartz composite sink with a cutting board from Franke.
8. A quartz resin sink from Kindred Industries.
9. A "Culinex 9090" sink from Porcher.
10. A triple bowl sink from Epic.
11. Blanco's octagon-shaped sink.
12. A sunshine yellow sink from American Standard.
13. The "Yorkshire" sink with cutting board from Eljer.
14. American Standard's "Silhouette" sink with accessories.
15. "Parisienne" sink from Eljer.
16. The Moenstone sink by Moen.

1.

2.

3.

5.

6.

7.

4.

9.

8.

10.

11.

12.

13.

14.

15.

16.

■ ■ ■ ■ ■ ■ ■ ■ ■ ■ ■ ■ ■ ■

Fixtures

■ ■ ■ ■ ■ ■ ■ ■ ■ ■ ■ ■ ■ ■

1. A goose-necked fixture with separate handle and spray wash from Artistic Brass.
2. A Kroin fixture.
3. A contemporary trio from Artistic Brass.
4. Epic's "Innovations" faucet with diamond handles and soap dispenser.
5. Moen's "Chateau" single-lever faucet.
6. Epic's "Classics" collection faucet and cross handles.
7 and 8. "Primrose" fixture from Eljer; 8 shows the above-counter mixer.
9. Watercolors "Sprint" series.
10. Watercolors Inc.'s "Regal Antique" series.
11. Antique French fixture with two handles and two spouts.
12. Horus's "Julia" fixture.
13. Victorian-style fixtures from Harrington.

1.

2.

3.

4.

5.

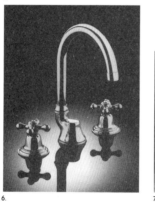
6.

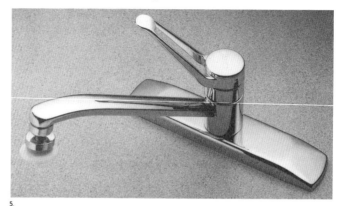
7.

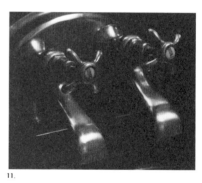

9.

1. Hansgrohe's "Duo" kitchen fixture.
2. A white enamel fixture from Watercolors Inc.
3. "Aragos" faucets with pull-out spray fixture from Porcher.
4. "Gemme" high spout kitchen and bar faucets.
5. The "Legend Riser" from Moen lifts ten inches above the sink.
6. NuTone's hot-water dispenser.
7. The "Contempra" automatic faucet by Water Facets operates by infrared sensor.
8. The "Ronda" single faucet by Hansa America.
9. Corianpoli series by Watercolors Inc. with a selection of cross handles.
10. The "Pull-Out" by Abbaka.
11. The "Heritage" faucet with cross handles and spray wash by American Standard.
12. A "KWCdome" single lever faucet with retractable hand spray.

1.

2.

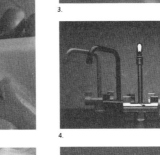

3.

4.

5.

6.

7.

8.

9.

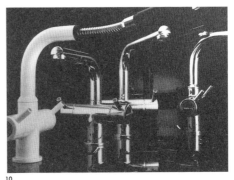

10.

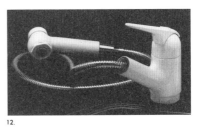

11.

12.

Cooktops

1. General Electric Monogram's cooktop system.
2. Jenn-Air's single cooktop grill element.
3. Dacor's "Quintessence" gas glass cooktop with its raised ventilation system.
4. Gaggenau's three-zone system with gas burners, electric deep fryer, and halogen zone.
5. Dacor's "Smooth Top Five Cooktop" with raised ventilation system.
6. Viking's built-in gas range top.
7. U.S. Range cooktop (see page 192).
8. Modern Maid's smooth-top quartz halogen/radiant cooktop.
9. General Electric/ Monogram's down-draft grill cooktop.
10. Broan's "Silhouette Range Hood" with tempered glass visor.
11. FiveStar's six-burner cooktop with griddle built-in.
12. Thermador's stainless-steel grill (see page 86).
13. Magic Chef's four-burner cooktop.
14. Gaggenau's six-burner cooktop.
15. Creda's Domino Cooktop series.

1.

4.

2.

10.

6.

3.

5.

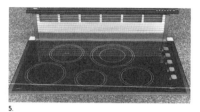

11.

7.

8.

9.

12.

13.

14.

15.

Stoves

1. A freestanding U.S. Range unit with six burners and one oven.
2. Thermador's Professional Range with dual ovens—one a convection—and burners fitted with S grates.
3. Viking's six-burner with griddle/summerplate and dual ovens from the Professional series.
4. Garland's six-burner dual oven with griddle.

5 and 6. Wolf's six-burner with dual ovens, in black and stainless-steel finishes.

7. Groen's Convection Combo Steamer Oven.
8. FiveStar's four-burner with single oven and griddle.
9. La Cornue's professional range with two gas burners, two electric burners, gas-fired barbecue with the "Plaque Coupe De Feu" and two convection ovens.
10. Vulcan's six-burner with single oven and storage space under the griddle.

2.

3.

1.

4.

5.

6.

7.

8.

9.

10.

Stoves and Hoods

1. Broan's "9000" series range hood.
2. Abbaka's Barrel Form Seamless cylinder shape hood.
3. Broan's Professional series range hood for residential use.
4. Abbaka's stainless-steel hood with utensil rail and *S* hooks.
5. Viking's stainless-steel hood.
6. A custom-designed hood.
7. A custom-designed hood.
8. A flip-out hood by Vent-A-Hood.
9. A combination cookstove and bake oven from Tulikivi.
10. An Elmira Sweet Heart woodburning stove.
11. A tandoori oven (see page 188).
12. An Aga Cookers stove with its four doors open.
13. An Aga Cookers stove.

1.

2.

3.

4.

5.

6.

7.

8.

9.

10.

11.

12.

13.

Ranges and Wall Ovens

1. Magic Chef's smooth-top electric range with Ceran cooking surface that uses regular pans.
2. General Electric's electric range with single oven.
3. Tappan's Upswept gas range.
4. Magic Chef's four-burner gas range with sealed burners.
5. Crown's six-burner, double-oven gas range.
6. General Electric's double electric burner with updraft venting grill.
7. Modern Maid's all-gas down-draft range.
8. Thermador's double convection/thermal wall oven.
9. General Electric/Monogram's double wall oven.
10. Magic Chef's built-in 30-inch gas wall oven/microwave combo with full-size oven capacity.
11. A vintage Magic Chef, circa 1930, from Antique Stove Heaven.
12. Refurbished and refinished in lilac and mint by Oven Arts.
13. A 1947 O'Keefe and Merritt Town & Country six-burner, three-oven stove from Antique Stove Heaven.
14. A 1930 "Reliable" stove from Antique Stove Heaven.
15. A "Quick Meal" six-burner, two-oven stove with broiler from Antique Stove Heaven.

1.

2.

3.

4.

5.

6.

7.

8.

9.

10.

11.

12.

13.

14.

15.

Refrigerators

1. Sub-Zero's 30 cubic feet side-by-side refrigerator/freezer with through-door ice and chilled water.
2. Amana's 24-inch-deep freestanding refrigerator.
3. Sub-Zero's built-in side-by-side refrigerator/freezer accepts custom-designed front panels.
4. An open view of Sub-Zero's side-by-side refrigerator/freezer with its award-winning interiors—rounded corners and fully adjustable shelves.

5 and 6. Modern Maid's 24-inch-deep side-by-side refrigerator/freezer—open and closed.

7 and 8. A Magic Chef's 23.5 cubic feet side-by-side refrigerator/freezer with through-door ice and chilled water—open and closed.

9. Gibson's upright freezer.

10 and 11. Gerald's undercounter jumbo upright freezer—open and closed.

12. Sub-Zero's under-counter refrigerator.

2.

3.

4.

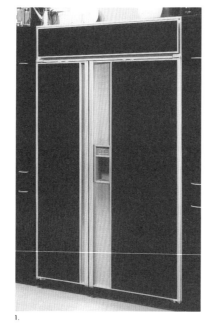

5.

6.

9.

1.

7.

8.

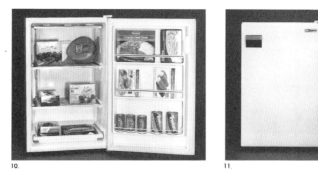

10.

11.

12.

Refrigerators

1. Traulsen's double glass door refrigerator/ freezer.
2. Traulsen's side-by-side refrigerator and freezer.
3. Traulsen double refrigerator with fruit and vegetable drawers on bottom.
4. Beverage-Air's double-width refrigeration with no internal wall dividers between the sides.
5. Beverage-Air's triple refrigerator/freezer on wheels.
6. Marvel's undercounter beverage center.
7. Marvel's undercounter wine grotto.
8. The Euroflair refrigerator/wine cooler imported by Frigidaire Appliances.
9. Vinothèque Mignon wine cellar from The Wine Enthusiast.

1.

2.

3.

4.

5.

6.

7.

8.

9.

269

1. A patterned floor of white oak and walnut (see page 26).
2. Inlaid diamond pattern of hickory and mahogany from Kentucky Wood Floors.
3. An inlaid mahogany border.
4. Old unfinished plank flooring in a barn kitchen (see page 64).
5. Old pine boards, simply finished (see page 126).
6. A plank floor painted in a checkerboard pattern (see page 138).
7. Wood borders for a tile floor.
8. A parquet floor with a urethane finish from Hartco.
9. A reproduction heating register from Renovators Supply.
10. Painted oak floor (see page 226).
11. Wide-planked pegged floor (see page 60).
12. "Winter white" Sterling Strip with double border of "Gunstock" Sterling Strip from Bruce Hardwood Floors.
13. "Natural" Sterling Prestige Planks from Bruce Hardwood Floors.
14. Diagonal accent of "Gunstock" Sterling Strip from Bruce Hardwood Floors.

1.

2.

3.

4.

5.

6.

7.

8.

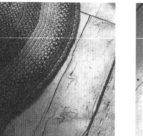

9.

10.

11.

12.

13.

14.

1. "Terralast" from Vpi (see page 158).
2. "Solid" from Armstrong Components.
3. "American Arts" Designer Solarian floor from Armstrong.
4. "Colonial Classic" Solarian flooring from Armstrong.
5. Vinyl flooring from Color Tile Inc.
6. "Quadrants" from Armstrong Components.
7. "TAOS" Designer Solarian II from Armstrong.
8. "Mardi Gras" Starstep Solarian from Armstrong.
9. "Carrara" Mannington Sterling from Mannington Resilient Floors.
10. Armstrong Components sunburst design by Sheila Lukins and Julee Rosso.
11. "Brighton Beach" Mannington Gold from Mannington Resilient Floors.

1.

2.

3.

4.

5.

6.

7.

8.

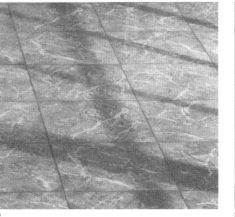

9.

10.

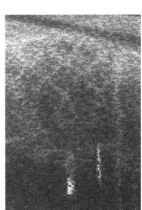

11.

271

1. A "Spanish MH" tile floor with a mosaic border from Country Floors.
2. The Sicis tile "I Cosmati" collection of marble stones, available from Hastings Tile & Il Bagno Collection.
3. Black-and-white diamond pattern ceramic floor.
4. "Creekstone" from American Olean.
5. Blue Crystal Gramitech floor tile.
6. Ceramic floor tile from Color Tile Inc.
7. Traditional white tile floor from American Olean.
8. Checkerboard ceramic tile from Color Tile Inc.
9. Italian floor tile with Pompeiian-style mosaic.
10. Mortarless brick floor.
11. Hexagonal terra-cotta tile.
12. Old brick floor with unusual accent tiles.
13. Reclaimed French floor tile.

1.

2.

3.

4.

5.

6.

7.

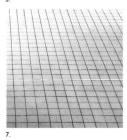

8.

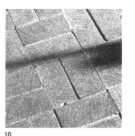

9.

10.

11.

12.

13.

1. Satin aluminum and glass pendant lamp from George Kovacs Lighting.
2. Pewter-finish halogen "chandelier" from George Kovacs Lighting.
3. Post-modern incandescent pendant lamp from George Kovacs Lighting.
4. The Pyrex diffuser in this halogen ceiling fixture distributes the light freely; designed by Gianfranco Frattini.
5. A structural-looking pendant fixture from George Kovacs Lighting.
6. Two suspension lamps from Lightolier.
7. A five-unit halogen suspension lamp from George Kovacs Lighting.
8. The "Trama" pendant lamp from Artemide.
9 and 11. The "Mikado" system designed by Porsche for Artemide.
10. Three incandescent suspension lamps from Lightolier.
12. A low-voltage suspension fixture designed by Vico Magistretti.

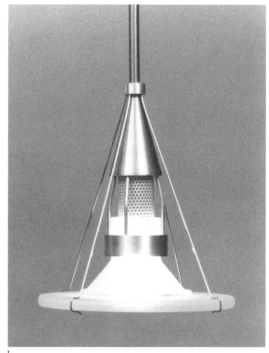

1.

2.

3.

4.

5.

6.

7.

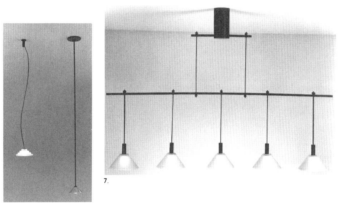

9.

8.

10.

11.

12.

Lighting

1. The "Celeste" ceiling lamp, designed by Ron Rezek for Artimede.
2. The "Opalume" ceiling lamps from Lightolier.
3. "Lumironde," a round fluorescent ceiling fixture from Lightolier.
4. "Egina" from Artemide.
5. "Gridworks" surface fluorescent lighting from Lightolier.
6. "Cascade" fixture from Artemide.
7. "Coffer-Lyte" recessed fluorescent lighting from Lightolier.
8. "Filo I," "Filo II," and "Gabbia" track lamp-holders from Halo.
9. "Colletto" and "Ombar" track lamp-holders from Halo.
10. A Robert Sonneman–designed wall lamp from George Kovacs Lighting.
11. "Lytrim" from Lightolier.
12. Lightolier's "Spotlight."
13. Lightolier's "Super Beamer" and "Geostar."
14. Track and spotlight lamps from Lightolier.

1.

2.

3.

4.

5.

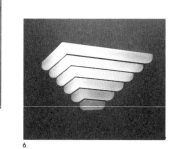

6.

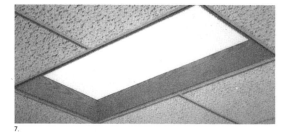

7.

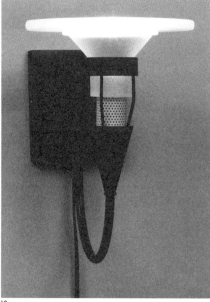

10.

8.

9.

11.

12.

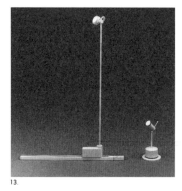

13.

14.

Tables and Chairs

1 and 2. Two glass-topped tables help create a natural look.

3. Neo-Biedermeier: The table is stainless steel and granite, the slipcovers are leather.

4. A marble and iron pedestal table.

5. A second table for intimate dinners.

6. Comfortable painted chairs surround an old round table.

7. A drop-leaf farmhouse table.

8. A cantilevered drawer becomes an impromptu table.

9. A Shaker-style table with bench and four chairs.

10. Slipcovered chairs around a country table.

11. A hammered wood table with "lightning bolt" corners.

12. Sturdy mismatched chairs around a well-worn table.

13. Custom-designed post-modern table with flea market chairs.

14. Andrée Putman–designed table with vintage 1930s Robert Mallet Stevens chairs.

15. Custom-designed chopping board.

1.

2.

3.

4.

5.

6.

7.

8.

9.

10.

11.

12.

13.

14.

15.

Flea Market Finds and Unusual Accessories

1. A copper stag basin from the flea market holds oversized wooden paddles.
2. A metal plate rack contains an assortment of baskets.
3. A whimsical brass bottle opener.
4. An antique tooled metal box holds sand and votive candles.
5. "Juicy Salif" designed by Philippe Starck for the Alessi Company.
6. A vintage chopping block, complete with its own knife.
7. An antique hand clasp holds notes.
8. A wooden tool box for mail and paraphernalia.
9. An old basket for potholders and oven mitts.
10. An antique scale.
11. A hanging Italian ceramic still life: trompe l'oeil caviar and toast.
12. A brass paper towel holder.
13. A wicker tray holds homemade vinegars, oils, and jams.
14. A spoon mobile.
15. "Max Le Chinois" colander designed by Philippe Starck for the Alessi Company.

1.

3.

4.

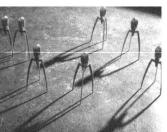

2.

5.

6.

7.

8.

9.

10.

11.

12.

13.

14.

15.

276

Cookbooks

1. Shelves built into the back of banquette seating.
2. Flea market paper cutter used as a cookbook holder.
3. Wall and cabinets devoted to built-in shelving.
4. Open shelving in a kitchen corner.
5. Sturdy shelving in a pantry is used for condiments and cookbooks.
6. A *metate* used as a cookbook holder.
7. Two small shelves on wooden brackets.
8. Craig Claiborne's cookbook library (see page 188).

1.

2.

3.

4.

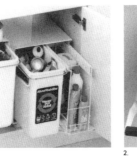
5.

6.

7.

8.

Recycling Tools

1. Blanco box system.
2. The Hold Everything can crusher.
3. Iron cabinet-door bag holder for lightweight recyclables.
4. The Hold Everything Curbside recycler.
5. The Hold Everything maple-top recycling cabinet.
6. Hold Everything recycling bins.
7. The Hold Everything wooden recycling unit.
8. A wood and twine newspaper recycler.

1. 2. 3. 4.

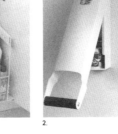
5.

6.

7.

8.

Gadgets for Special Needs

1. "Jiffy" glass brush attaches to the sink bottom by suction.
2. A gripper for opening screw-top bottle caps.
3. A bottle vise.
4. A gripper for stove knobs.
5. This cork-topped trivet is equipped with wheels.
6. Bread-slicing jig; the bread knife has an easy-grip handle.
7. A walker tray.
8. Stationary cheese grater.
9. Flatware with grippers.
10. Cup caddy for walkers and wheelchairs.
11. Easy-grip chopper.
12. Utensil gripper.
13. Non-skid paring board.
14. Tip-proof soup bowl.

Information on all these products is available through Bissell Healthcare, P.O. Box 3697, Grand Rapids, MI 49501.

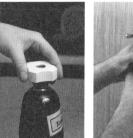

1.

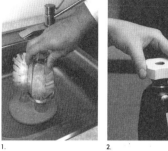

2.

3.

4.

5.

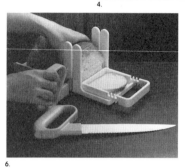

6.

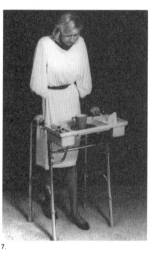

7.

8.

9.

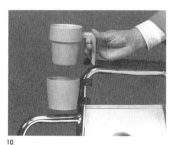

10.

11.

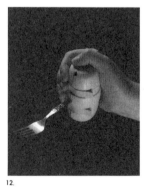

12.

13.

14.

Directory

Manufacturers

Abbaka
435 23rd Street
San Francisco, CA 94107
1-800-548-3932

Admiral Home Appliances
740 King Edward Avenue
Cleveland, TN 37311
615-472-3371

Aga Cookers Inc.
RFD 1, Box 477
Stowe, VT 05672
802-253-9727

The Alessi Company
c/o The Marcus Group
10 Wheeling Avenue
Woburn, MA 01801

Allmilmo Corp.
P.O. Box 629, 70 Clinton Road
Fairfield, NJ 07004-2976
201-227-2502

Amana Refrigeration
Amana, IA 52204
1-800-843-0304

American Olean Tile Co.
100 Cannon Avenue
Lansdale, PA 19446
215-855-1111

American Standard, Inc.
1 Centennial Plaza
P.O. Box 6820
Piscataway, NJ 08855-6820
201-980-3000

American Woodmark Corp.
3102 Shawnee Drive
P.O. Box 1990
Winchester, VA 22601
1-800-388-2483

Amsterdam Corporation
150 E. 58th Street
New York, NY 10155
212-644-1350

Armstrong World Industries
P.O. Box 3001
Lancaster, PA 17604
1-800-233-3823

Artemide Lighting
1980 New Highway
Farmingdale, NY 11735
516-694-9292

Artistic Brass
4100 Ardmore Avenue
South Gate, CA 90280
1-800-877-4100

Avonite
5100 Goldleaf Parkway
Suite 200
Los Angeles, CA 90056
1-800-4-AVONITE

Baldwin Hardware Corp.
841 East Wyomissing Boulevard
P.O. Box 15048
Reading, PA 19612
215-777-7811

Barclay Products
4000 Porrett Drive
Gurnee, IL 60031-1246
708-244-1234

Beverage Air
700 Buffington Road
Highway I 85
Spartansburg, SC 29303
803-582-8111

Blanco
1001 Lower Landing Road
Suite 607
Blackwood, NJ 08012
1-800-451-5782

Boffi Arredamento Cucina, SPA
Via G Oberdan
20030 Lentate Sul Seveso
Milan, Italy

Broadway Industries
The Broadway Collection
250 N. Troost
Olathe, KS 66061
1-800-766-1661

Broan Mfg. Co.
P.O. Box 140
926 W. State Street
Hartford, WI 53027
414-673-4340

Bruce Hardwood Floors
16803 Dallas Parkway
Dallas, TX 75248
1-800-722-4647

Busby-Gilbert Tile Co.
16021 Arminta Street
Van Nuys, CA 91406
818-780-9460

Calphalon
Commercial Aluminum
    Cookware Co.
Dept 55
P.O. Box 583
Toledo, Ohio 43693

Casson Lessard
RD 5, Province Line Road
Princeton, NJ 08540

The Chicago Faucet Co.
2100 S. Nuclear Drive
Des Plaines, IL 60018

Color Tile
515 Houston Street
Fort Worth, TX 76102
817-870-9538

Cooper Lighting
P.O. Box 4446
Houston, TX 77210
713-739-5400

Corian Products
DuPont Co.
PPD Dept.
Wilmington, DE 19898
1-800-4-CORIAN

Creda Inc.
5700 West Touhy Avenue
Chicago, IL 60648
708-647-6917

Dacor
950 S. Raymond Avenue
Pasadena, CA 91109-7202
818-799-1000

Dean/U.S. Range Inc.
14501 S. Broadway
Gardena, CA 90248
213-770-8800

Digitool Co.
Box 12350
Aspen, CO 81611
303-925-8177

DuPont Corian
G-52050
P.O. Box 80010
Wilmington, DE 19880
1-800-426-7426

Eljer Industries
901 10th Street
Plano, TX 75074
1-800-PL-ELJER

Elkay
2222 Camden Court
Oak Brook, IL 60521

Elmira Woodburning Stoves
Hartland Appliances, Inc.
5 Hoffman Street
Kitchener, ON N2M 3M5
Canada
519-743-8111

Epic
55 E. 111th Street
Indianapolis, IN 46280
317-848-1812

Epro, Inc.
156 East Broadway
Westerville, OH 43081
614-882-6990

Euroflaire by Frigidaire
6000 Perimeter Drive
Dublin, OH 43017
1-800-365-1365

Fivestar
c/o Brown Stove Works, Inc.
P.O. Box 2490
Cleveland, TN 37320

Florida Tile
A Division of Premark
P.O. Box 447
Lakeland, FL 33802
1-800-352-8453

Formica Corporation
10155 Reading Road
Cincinnati, OH 45241
513-786-3533

Franke
Kitchen Systems Division
212 Church Road
North Wales, PA 19454-4140
1-800-626-5771

Frigidaire
(A Division of WCI Major
   Appliance Group)
6000 Perimeter Drive
Dublin, OH 43017
1-800-451-7007
■

Gaggenau
425 University Avenue
Norwood, MA 02062
617-255-1766

Garland Consumer Products
185 E. South Street
Freeland, PA 18004

General Electric
GE Appliances
Appliance Park
Louisville, KY 40225
1-800-626-2000

George Kovacs Lighting, Inc.
67-25 Otto Road
Glendale, NY 11385
718-392-8190

Gerald Industries
16390 N.W. 52nd Avenue
Miami Lakes, FL 33014

Gibson
(A Division of WCI Major
   Appliance Group)
600 Perimeter Drive
Dublin, Ohio 43017
1-800-458-1445

The Granitech Corp.
600 S. 23rd Street
P.O. Box 1780
Fairfield, IA 52556-1780
515-472-6161

Green Street Details
2133 NW York
Portland, OR 97210
1-800-275-7855

Groen
1900 Pratt Boulevard
Elk Grove Village, IL 60007
708-439-2400

Grohe
900 Lively Boulevard
Wood Dale, IL 60191
■

Halo Lighting
6 W. 20th Street
New York, NY 10011
212-645-4580

Hansa America
931 W. 19th Street
Chicago, IL 60608

Harrington Brass Works
166 Coolidge Avenue
Englewood, NJ 07631
201-871-6011

Hartco
900 S. Gay Street
Suite 2102
Knoxville, TN 37902
615-637-8234

Hastings Tile
Il Bagno Collection
30 Commercial Street
Freeport, NY 11520
516-379-3500

Hettich America, L.P.
12428 Sam Neely Road
P.O. Box 7664
Charlotte, NC 28241
704-588-6666

Hunter Douglas Inc.
2 Parkway, Route 17 South
Upper Saddle River, NJ 07458
■

Inch Mate
c/o DigiTool Corp.
Box 12350
Aspen, CO 81612
1-800-543-8930

In-Sink-Erator
Emerson Electric Co.
4700 21 Street
Racine, WI 53406

Inter Metro Industries Corp.
N. Washington Street
P.O. Box A
Wilkes-Barre, PA 18705-0557
717-825-2741

Italian Tile Center
Division of Italian Trade
   Commission
499 Park Avenue
New York, NY 10022
212-980-1500
■

JADO Bath & Hardware
   Mfg. Co.
P.O. Box 1329
1690 Calle Quetzal
Camarillo, CA 93011

Jenn-Air
3035 Shadeland
Indianapolis, IN 46226

■
Kentucky Wood Floors
P.O. Box 33726
Louisville, KY 40232
1-800-235-5235

KitchenAid
701 Main Street
St. Joseph, MI 49085

Kohler Co.
Kohler, WI 53044
414-457-1271

Kraft
306 E. 61st Street
New York, NY 10021
212-838-2214

KraftMaid Cabinetry
P.O. Box 1055
16052 Industrial Parkway
Middlefield, OH 44062
216-632-5333

Kroin
180 Fawcett Street
Cambridge, MA 02138
617-492-4000

KWC
1559 Sunland Lane
Costa Mesa, CA 92626
714-557-1933
■

La Cornue
c/o Purcell Murray Co.
113 Park Lane
Brisbane, CA 94005

Lightolier Inc.
100 Lighting Way
Secaucus, NJ 07096
201-864-3000
■

Magic Chef Co.
740 King Edward Avenue
Cleveland, TN 37311
615-472-3371

Mannington Resilient Floors
P.O. Box 30
Salem, NJ 08079
609-935-3000

Marvel Industries
233 Industrial Parkway
P.O. Box 997
Richmond, IN 47375-0997
1-800-428-6644

Mepla, Inc.
909 W. Market Center Drive
P.O. Box 1469
High Point, NC 27261-1469

Modern Maid
403 N. Main Street
Topton, PA 19562-1499
215-682-4211

Moen
377 Woodland Avenue
Elyria, OH 44036
216-323-3341
■

Nevamar Corp.
8339 Telegraph Road
Odenton, MD 21113
301-551-5000

NuTone
Madison & Red Bank Roads
Cincinnati, OH 45227
1-800-543-8687
■

Outwater Plastics Industries
4 Passaic Street
Wood Ridge, NJ 07075
1-800-888-0880

Oven Arts
P.O. Box 1633
Pacific Palisades, CA 90272
■

Palecek
P.O. Box 225, Station A
Richmond, CA 94808-0225
1-800-274-7730

Pero Group
34 Wildwood Road
New Rochelle, NY 10804
914-834-1182

Plexability
200 Lexington Avenue
Suite 506
New York, NY 10016

Poggenpohl, U.S., Inc.
5905 Johns Road
Tampa, FL 33634

Porcher
13-160 Merchandise Mart
Chicago, IL 60654
312-923-0995
■

Quaker Maid
A Division of WCI
Route 61
Leesport, PA 19533
215-926-3011
■

Rev-A-Shelf
2409 Plantside Drive
Jeffersontown, KY 40299
1-800-626-1126

Rutt Custom Cabinetry
HARROW Industries, Inc.
1564 Main Street
P.O. Box 129
Goodville, PA 17528
215-445-6751
∎

The St. Charles Companies
1401 Greenbrier Parkway, Suite 200
Chesapeake, VA 23320
804-424-3900

SieMatic
886 Town Center Drive
Langhorne, PA 19047
215-750-1928

Smallbone, Inc.
886 Town Center Drive
Langhorne, PA 19047
215-750-1928

Snaidero International USA
201 West 132 Street
Los Angeles, CA 90061

Sub-Zero Freezer Co.
P.O. Box 4130
4717 Hammersley Road
Madison, WI 53711
1-800-222-7820

Swedish Rehab—Division of Lumex
100 Spence Street
Bay Shore, NY 11706
1-800-645-5272
∎

Tappan
c/o WCI Major Appliance Co.
6000 Perimeter Drive
Dublin, Ohio 43017

Thermador
5119 District Boulevard
Los Angeles, CA 90040
213-562-1133

Thomas Industries
P.O. Box 7849
Louisville, KY 40207
1-800-825-5844

Timberlake Cabinet Co.
3102 Shawnee Drive
P.O. Box 1990
Winchester, VA 22601
1-800-388-2483

Traulsen & Co., Inc.
114-02 15th Avenue
College Point, NY 11356
1-800-542-4022

Tulikivi
The New Alberene Stone Co.
P.O. Box 300
Schuyler, VA 22969
∎

U.S. Range
14501 S. Broadway
Gardena, CA 90248
∎

Valle & Columbo, USA
1540 Highland Avenue
Duarte, CA 91010

Velux-America Inc.
P.O. Box 5001
Greenwood, SC 29648

Vermont Marble Co.
61 Main Street
Proctor, VT 05765
1-800-451-4468

Viking Range Corp.
111 Front Street
Greenwood, MS 38930
601-455-1200

Vpi
Vinyl Plastics, Inc.
3123 S. 9th Street
Sheboygan, WI 53081
1-800-874-4240

Vulcan
Food Service Equipment
P.O. Box 696
Louisville, KY 40201
502-778-2791
∎

Water Facets
3001 Redhill
Bldg. 5, Suite 108/145
Costa Mesa, CA 92626
1-800-243-4H2O

Waterford Irish Stoves, Inc.
16 Air Park Road #3
West Lebanon, NH 03784-9701
1-800-828-5781

WCI Major Appliance Group
116 E. Corporate Boulevard
Middlesex Business Park
South Plainfield, NJ 07080

Wenczel Tile Co.
200 Enterprise Ave.
Trenton, NJ 08638
609-599-4503

West World Imports
171 E. California Boulevard
Pasadena, CA 91105
818-449-8565

Whirlpool Appliance Group
2000 M-63
Benton Harbor, MI 49022
1-800-253-1301

WILSONART
Ralph Wilson Plastics Co.
600 General Bruce Drive
Temple, TX 76501
1-800-433-3222

Wolf Range Co.
19600 S. Alameda Street
Compton, CA 90221
310-637-3737

∎ ∎ ∎ ∎ ∎ ∎ ∎ ∎ ∎ ∎ ∎

Suppliers: Retail Outlets, Catalogs, Craftsmen, and More

∎ ∎ ∎ ∎ ∎ ∎ ∎ ∎ ∎ ∎ ∎

ABC Carpet & Home
888 Broadway
New York, NY 10003
212-473-3000

adaptAbility Catalog
P.O. Box 515
Colchester, CT 06415-0515
1-800-243-9232

Antique Stove Heaven
5414 Southwestern Avenue
Los Angeles, CA 90062
213-298-5581

Asko Asea
903 N. Bowser, Suite 200
Richardson, TX 75081
214-644-8595

Attitudes Catalogue
1213 Elko Drive
Sunnyvale, CA 94089
1-800-525-2468
∎

Ballard Designs Catalogue
1670 DeFoor Avenue NW
Atlanta, GA 30318
404-351-5099

The Barefoot Contessa
Main Street
East Hampton, NY 11937

Barney's New York
106 Seventh Avenue
New York, NY 10011
212-929-9000

Bering Home Center
6102 Westheimer
Houston, TX 77057
713-785-6400

Bode's General Store
P.O. Box 100
Abiquiu, NM 87510
505-685-4422

Bowery Discount Hardware & Restaurant Supply
105 The Bowery
New York, NY 10002
212-966-6375

Bridge Co. (Kitchen Warehouse)
214 E. 52 Street
New York, NY 10022
212-688-4220

Brinton's
546 Carmel Rancho Shopping Center
Carmel, CA 93923
408-624-8541

Bristol Farms
606 Fair Oaks Avenue
S. Pasadena, CA 91030
818-441-5450

Broadway Panhandler
520 Broadway
New York, NY 10012
212-966-0120

Brown & Jenkins Trading Co. Catalog
Box 1570
Burlington, VT 05402
1-800-456-5282
∎

C & W Mercantile
Main Street
Bridgehampton, NY 11932

A Catalog for Cooks
c/o Williams-Sonoma
P.O. Box 7456
San Francisco, CA 94120
1-800-541-2233 (Call for catalog
   and store nearest you)

Chamber's Catalog
P.O. Box 7841
San Francisco, CA 94120
1-800-334-9790

The Chef's Catalogue
3215 Commercial Avenue
Northbrook, IL 60662-1900

Claiborne Gallery
558 Canyon Road
Santa Fe, NM 87501
505-982-8019

Chris Collicott
1151½ N. La Brea Avenue
Los Angeles, CA 90038
213-876-5112

Colonial Garden Kitchens
   Catalog
P.O. Box 66
Hanover, PA 17333
717-633-3330

Community Kitchens
The Art of Food Catalogue
P.O. Box 2311, Dept. GN
Baton Rouge, LA 70821-2311
1-800-535-9901

Conran's Habitat
160 E. 54th Street
New York, NY 10003
1-800-3-CONRAN

Country Floors
15 E. 16th Street
New York, NY 10003

Country Gear Ltd.
Main Street
Bridgehampton, NY 11932
516-537-1032

Coyote Café General Store
   Catalog
132 W. Water Street
Santa Fe, NM 87501
505-982-2454

Crate and Barrel Catalogue
P.O. Box 3057
Northbrook, IL 60065-3057

Veva Crozer
19 Rockwood
Greenwich, CT 06830
203-661-5476
∎

Dean & DeLuca
560 Broadway
New York, NY 10012

Domaine
661-120th NE
Bellevue, WA 98006
206-450-9900

Downsview Kitchens
2635 Rena Road
Mississauga, ON L4T 1G6
Canada

G. R. Durenberger Antiques
31531 Camino Capistrano
San Juan Capistrano, CA 92675
∎

East Hampton Florist & Country
   Store
66 Newton Lane
East Hampton, NY 11937

The Eclectic Shop
214 E. 70th Street
New York, NY 10021

Elizabeth's Market Garden
144 Camino Escondido
Santa Fe, NM 87501
505-982-4149

Enrichments for Better Living
   Catalog
145 Tower Drive
P.O. Box 579
Hinsdale, IL 60521
1-800-323-5547

Judith Ets-Hokin
3525 California Street
San Francisco, CA 94118
415-668-3191

Everyday Gourmet
2905 Old Canton Road
Jackson, MS 39216
601-362-0723
∎

Fine Pottery
Dora Tse Pe Pena
San Ildefonso
P.O. Box 3679
Santa Fe, NM 87501-0679
505-455-7560
or 505-455-7461

Fishs Edy
889 Broadway
New York, NY 10003
212-420-9020

Forrest-Jones
3274 Sacramento Street
San Francisco, CA 94115
415-567-2483

Fortune's Almanac
150 Chestnut Street
San Francisco, CA 94111-1004
1-800-331-2300

Fred Sammons Catalog
145 Tower Drive
Burr Ridge, IL 60521
1-800-323-5547
∎

Gardener's Eden Catalogue
P.O. Box 7307
San Francisco, Ca 94120-7307
1-800-541-2233

Gardener's Supply Company
   Catalogue
128 Intervale Road
Burlington, VT 05401
802-863-1700

Greenbrier Gourmet
Greenbrier Hotel
White Sulphur Springs, WV
   24896
304-536-1110
∎

Hammacher Schlemmer
   Catalogue
9180 Le Saint Drive
Fairfield, OH 45014
800-543-3366

Hard-To-Find-Tools Catalogue
5 Vose Farm Road
P.O. Box 803
Peterborough, NH 03460-0803
603-924-9541

Harry & David's Country Store
2836 S Pacific Highway
Medford, OR 97501
503-776-2277

H.M.S. Pinafore Ltd.
15 Purchase Street
Rye, NY 10580
914-921-2327

Hold Everything Catalog
P.O. Box 7807
San Francisco, CA 94120-7807
1-800-541-2233

The Home Depot
2727 Paces Ferry Road
Atlanta, GA 30339
404-433-8211

Home Town
131 Wooster Street
New York, NY 10012
212-674-5770

Home Trends Catalog
779 Mt. Read Boulevard
Rochester, NY 14606
716-254-6520

The Horchow Collection
P.O. Box 620048
Dallas, TX 75262-0048
1-800-395-5397

Howard Kaplan Antiques
827 Broadway
New York, NY 10003
212-674-1000
∎

Ikea US Inc.
Plymouth Commons
Plymouth Meeting, PA 19462
412-747-0747

Independent Living Aids
   Catalog
27 East Mall
Plainview, NY 11803
1-800-537-2118

Indigo Seas
123 N. Robertson Boulevard
Los Angeles, CA 90048
∎

Joan Cook Housewares
   Catalogue
3200 S.E. 14 Avenue
Ft. Lauderdale, FL 33350
800-327-3799
∎

Kindred Industries
1000 Kindred Road
Midland, ON LAR 4K9
Canada
1-800-465-5586

Sue Fisher King
3067 Sacramento Street
San Francisco, CA 94115

The King Arthur Flour
  Baker's Catalogue
RR 2 Box 56
Norwich, VT 05055
1-800-827-6836

Kitchen & Bath Source Book
  (annual)
MBC Data Distribution
  Publications
3901 West 86th Street, Suite 330
Indianapolis, IN 46268
317-875-7776

Kitchen Concepts Inc.
265 Halstead Avenue
Harrison, NY 10528
914-835-0521

Kitchen Etc.
US Route 1, Lafayette Road
N. Hampton, NH 03862
603-929-1137

Kitchen Glamour
26770 Grand River Avenue
Detroit, MI 48240
313-537-1300
▪
Le Cordon Bleu at Trump
  Tower
725 Fifth Avenue
New York, NY 10022
212-308-4067

Lillian Vernon Catalogue
Virginia Beach, VA 23479-0002
804-430-1500
▪
Macy's The Cellar
151 West 34th Street
New York, NY 10001

Markline Catalogue
P.O. Box 8
Elmira, NY 14902
1-800-225-8390

Miele Appliances
22D Worlds Fair Drive
Somerset, NJ 08873

Museum Collections Catalogue
921 Eastwind Drive
Westerville, OH 43081-3341
1-800-442-2460
▪

Ogletree's Machine Shop
1027 Pope Street
St. Helena, CA 94574
707-963-3537

Oren's Daily Roast
1574 First Avenue
New York, NY 10028
212-737-2690
▪
Plow and Hearth Catalogue
301 Madison Road
Orange, VA 22960
800-627-1712

Pottery Barn
P.O. Box 7044
San Francisco, CA 94120-7044
1-800-922-5507 (call for location
  of stores and for catalog)
▪
Real Goods Trading Corp.
  Catalogue
966 Mazzoni Street
Ukiah, CA 95482
1-800-762-7325

Reliable Home Office Catalogue
P.O. Box 804117
Chicago, IL 60680-9968

Renovator's Supply
Renovator's Old Mill
Millers Falls, MA 01349
1-800-659-2211

The Restaurant Store
Division of Westchester
  Restaurant Supply Co.
Route 9A
Elmsford, NY 10523
1-800-552-5223

Richard Mulligan Antiques
8157 Sunset Boulevard
Los Angeles, CA 90046
213-650-8660

Round Hearth Garden Center &
  Florist Inc.
199 Fort Pond Boulevard
East Hampton, NY 11937
516-324-2056
▪
St. George's Dinnerware
119 St. George Street
St. Augustine, FL 32084
904-829-6773

Sample House
4722 Bengal
Dallas, TX 75235
214-688-0751

Sears, Roebuck and Co.
Sears Tower
Chicago, IL 60684
1-800-741-2568

Second Hand Rose
270 Lafayette Street
New York, NY 10012
212-431-7673

Shabby Chic
1013 Montana Avenue
Santa Monica, CA 90403
310-394-1975

Shabby Chic
93 Greene Street
New York, NY 10010
212-274-9842

Shelly Tile
979 Third Avenue
New York, NY 10022

Solutions Catalog
P.O. Box 6878
Portland, OR 97228
1-800-342-9988

Summer Hill Ltd.
934A Santa Cruz Avenue
Menlo Park, CA 94025
415-363-2600

Sundance Catalogue
780 West Layton Avenue
Salt Lake City, UT 84104
1-800-422-2770

Sunstruct Co. Inc.
31C Ponquogue Avenue
Hampton Bays, NY 11946

Sur La Table
84 Pine Street
Seattle, WA 98101
206-448-2244
▪
Terra Cotta
11925 Montana
Los Angeles, CA 90049
310-826-7878

Tilecraft Ltd.
438 W. Francisco Boulevard
San Rafael, CA 94901
415-456-0282

Trompe L'Oeil—The Painted
  Look
Nicki Caplan
1537 Benedict Canyon
Beverly Hills, CA 90210
213-653-1322

Vermont Country Store Catalog
P.O. Box 3000
Manchester Center, VT
  05255-3000
802-362-2400
▪
Watercolors, Inc.
Garrison, NY 10524
914-424-3327

Westchester Marble and Granite
610 S. Fulton Avenue
Mt. Vernon, NY 10550
1-800-634-0866

Williams-Sonoma Catalog
P.O. Box 7456
San Francisco, CA 94120-7456
1-800-541-2233

Williams-Sonoma Outlet
231 Tenth Avenue
New York, NY 10011
212-206-8118

The Wine Enthusiast
P.O. Box 39
Pleasantville, NY 10570

Winterthur Museum and
  Gardens Catalogue
Dover, DE 19901
1-800-767-0500

Wolfman Gold & Good
  Company
116 Greene Street
New York, NY 10012
212-431-1888

The Wooden Spoon Catalogue
P.O. Box 931
Clinton, CT 06413-0931
1-800-431-2207

Wood-Mode, Inc.
1 Second Street
Kreamer, PA 17833
717-374-2711

Worldly Goods Gift Shop
52 Purchase Street
Rye, NY 10580
914-967-1770
▪
Zabar's Catalogue
2245 Broadway
New York, NY 10024
212-496-1234

Zona
97 Greene Street
New York, NY 10012

Index

Page numbers in boldface refer to captions.